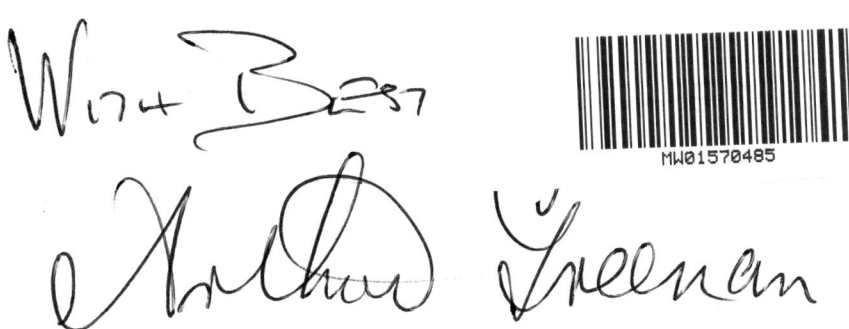

From the Heights

of

Drylaw Hill

by

Arthur Greenan

Published by Linton Brig Publications

Copyright © Arthur Greenan 2008

First Imprint February 2008

ISBN: 978-0-9558124-0-8

arthur.greenan@tiscali.co.uk

Acknowledgements

I acknowledge copyright and ownership of three items. The first is the photo of the Clydesdale stallion, by Kate Stephen of The Clydesdale Horse Society. The second is the photo of the painting 'Ploughing' by Eirene Hunter. The third is the ad verbatim use of the obituary of James Cameron by the Scotsman newspaper.

I am grateful to Nick Melville, the highly respected and published poet and Debbie Miller, the renowned author for their help. They were a great source of inspiration to me. The guidance, practical advice and time which they also availed to me was quite unbelievable!

I am truly indebted to them both.

Arthur Greenan

East Linton

Scotland

Sunday, 11th November 2007.

Dedication

To

Sally,

For her love, her quiet but consistent support

and

her infectious laughter in moments of adversity.

She looks as she cooks.

Quite exquisite!

Contents

Drylaw Hill	3
Part One	6
The Heights of Drylaw Hill	8
When Winter Comes	11
The Old Rugged Horse	15
The Red Cross Horse Parade	36
The Horse Whisperers	38
St Peter's Stable	49
The Acorn and the Oak	51
Star Looks Down	54
Brother to the Ox	59
The Dying Ploughman	65
Part Two	67
The Miner's Story	69
Pate's Kilt	75
Welsh Courage	78
The Black and White Minstrel	85
Dod Scott, the Miner	91
The Coming of the Light	97
Part Three	105
Phallic Symbolism	108
Judge Laurie Tinderwood	112
The Honorarium	116
A Rose by Any Other Name	118
The Canon and the Curate	121
The Roses of Haddington	127

The Cardinal's Cucumber	134
Ladybird	141
Part Four	147
The Black Holocaust	148
The Black Holocaust, an epilogue.	155
Prof. John P. Mackintosh MP	159

Drylaw Hill

Drylaw Hill is a fertile, volcanic spine which forms the northern border of the small township of East Linton on the east coast of Scotland. The hill is traversed by a steep, winding country road that shoots down the other side, past Janefield, then onto North Berwick.

As a simple-minded country laddie I have always been deeply conscious of my roots. East Lothian, once the garden of Scotland, is my native county. It is my kingdom. Its people are my people. This came home to me with resounding clarity when Jenny, my horse who figures in the poem St Peter's Stable, was stabled for a year on the top of Drylaw Hill.

Each autumn evening, just before darkness fell, I went to feed her. A flock of a thousand starlings congregated on a single maple tree for their daily conference then they swished off around the parish of Prestonkirk. Across the heights of Drylaw Hill they soared, weaving black swirling ribbons throughout the turquoise sky. They then dipped and disappeared into the simmering orange inferno of the setting sun as it too descended into hiding behind the Garleton hills.

In the morning, the sun rose above Dunbar casting down its spring warmth upon the two of us. As Jenny munched her feed I became aware that I could view every feature of my cherished universe from the heights of Drylaw Hill. In that complete circle I could see Belhaven Bay, Dunbar Parish Church and a hint of The Holy Isle in the far distance. From Traprain Law to Hailes Castle, Nunraw Abbey to Lammer Law onto the Moorfoot Hills, Pentland Hills, Arthur's Seat, Edinburgh Castle, Forth Bridges with the Campsie Hills beyond them. Rising from the floor of the shimmering Firth of Forth are the Lomond Hills which are so symmetrical as to be known as 'The Paps o' Fife.' The coastline sweeps on past Falkland Palace to disappear towards St Andrews.

As we step back onto the southern shore we are overshadowed by the pinnacle of North Berwick Law, the ruin of Tantallon Castle and the bird sanctuary of the Bass Rock. We scan round by Whitekirk Church, once torched by the suffragettes, then homewards up the Janefield brae to the top of Drylaw Hill.

That is my land, my native land, my home for forty years.

Part One

The purpose of recording these stories was twofold. The first was to create a remembrance of the way we were and it is also a heartfelt tribute to the many resilient people that I have met as I have stumbled along the rocky path of life.

Each story is based on a true happening. To preserve the identity or to save any hurt, I have, where appropriate, changed the location, names of individuals, or both. Other stories are a composite of kindred events which lie well together as we see in 'The Horse Whisperers.'

The Rev. A Walker published a poem entitled 'The Dying Ploughboy' which may well be the original from which a number of regional variants such as The Dying Ploughman sprang. This was recited to me, whilst a schoolboy hurling upon a hay bogey at the Myles farm in 1952, by horseman, Harry Henderson.

The Rev Walker's work reminds me of a pre-requiem prayer.

This colloquial interpretation of the late Harry Henderson seems much more appreciative of a ploughman's life. Hence, I have chosen it to include.

The Heights of Drylaw Hill

Preston Mill
One of the twelve working mills driven by the River Tyne
in East Lothian in the 1820's

From the misty Moorfoot mountains, to the heights of Drylaw hill
The dewdrops slowly gather into a rolling trill
With trickling sons and daughters, from left and right they come
Fluming in together they head for *Tyninghame*

She flows towards Pencaitland, where *Glen Kinchie* draws its dram
Silent onto *Nisbet*, sair poached by Ted and Tam
With two mills passed and ten to come, she gathers strength and run
In the glade of Winton castle, she hails the Donort burn

She meanders into Haddington, powering *Abbey* and *Millfield*
Cascades the weir tae *Stevenson*, tae beild at *Sandy's* mill
The wintry plains of *Amisfield* give all to nature's drain
In the drouthy months o' summer, they suck it back again

At Hailes, she saw Queen Mary seduce her lover braw
She wept for rakish Darnley, sword through him, in the snaw
She's wrocht nine birlin' water wheels, as she snakes along her bed
In sight, is noo, the *Houston* mill but she is far from dead

She gurgles ower the shallow stanes, afore auld Linton brig
In deep pool she assembles, then pours forth a' her micht
She batters o'er the scarred Linn rocks, wi' treachery and sound
Her swirling hidden vortex where pair Dalgleish wis drowned

She roars across the dookit field, where auld Wull kept his doos
Gouging at the willows, where Myra grazed her coos
Ah! *Preston* mill, then yin mair drive, the burns cling to her breast
She's Tyne mouth bound to freedom, *Knowes* mill gives her rest!

The Linn rocks and the Tyne Brig at East Linton

When Winter Comes

We suddenly become aware that winter is descending upon us when we accept that the clocks have to be changed. In the autumn, they fall back, at least in America! What really seems to hit our consciousness is that the daylight shrinks and those dreich winter nights envelop us. Not so for the young people who cannot wait for those dark nights in which to scatter their hormones out of public gaze. Such desperation! I remember it well. Gone, but not forgotten.

But what of the elderly, the non-ambulant, the self-respecting poor and those who sleep in the doorways of posh city shops. What will winter mean to them? Is it not the hallmark of any civilised society that it cares for those least mentally and physically able to withstand the rigours of normal living?

As autumn closes and we sense that winter is gearing up to its full ferocity other indicators pop up. The Virginia creeper melds from olive green to a flushing red. Elm leaves become a vibrant translucent lemon. A robin with pouted orange breast dives in for a quick bath and is now ready to fight the world for his feeding patch. The chaffinches, blackbirds, starlings and magpies, emboldened with hunger, still have to run little red robin's gauntlet.

Thousands of weary geese flop into the fields of Hedderwick farm for a first bite after their epic journey from the Arctic Circle. It is a flight guided by instinct, fuelled by courage. They fire-up the ire of the grain farmer who sees his young blades of wheat puddled by two thousand webbed feet just as they were gathering enough size to remain standing in the face of the icy blasts.

In early autumn the horses need an extra bite to give them a bit of flesh with which to face the winter. As the temperature drops to six degrees the grass just stops growing. They fluff out their hair at an angle of forty-five degrees and turn their tails into the biting winds to retain their body heat. Another sure indicator is when, in the morning, the horses are clean despite the muddy field going hard with frost. Old horsemen know that it was too cold even for the beasts to lye down. Rather, they had slept standing but with their legs locked-in all night. It is now time to give them a dry bed inside a stable at night.

With the frost, horses, cows, deer and birds try to drink from the frozen trough. Surrounded by woodland we baled water from a running burn to give them a drink. In the stillness we heard footsteps in the wood. Not a bob-tailed deer, not a living soul was seen. Frosted, silvered leaves thudded onto the forest floor.

'What now?' we asked Donald, the hill shepherd. He had released twenty Blackface rams onto the hill. It was November 20th. With care and an extra daily bite of hay throughout the winter, his two thousand ewes would each give birth to a lamb, perhaps twins, in six months time and in the warmth of the spring time. Their first appearance on this earth would be the April 20th. In four weeks time, the shortest, darkest day of the year will arrive and with it, our hopes for a new year as we all sing:-

'O come all ye faithful, joyful and triumphant.'

Shepherd, Donald Dickson with David Lange, Prime Minister of New Zealand and Arthur Greenan, Prestonpans, 1986.

Will the elderly dodge hypothermia with a better heating allowance? Will those whose bodies are wracked with pain from manual labour be able to afford to retire on time? Will the down and outs in our cities survive this winter to enjoy the spirit of springtime. Will those who have their dishonest snouts in every public trough ever find their greed sated?

Perhaps we will dream of reincarnation as a Blackface sheep on the Lammermuir hills. Warm, fed and protected by Donald Dickson, their Good Shepherd of John's Cleugh!

The Old Rugged Horse

By 1955, the year I started to work with Bobby at East Windygoul farm, the twelve-horse stable had withered to five. The two old green Fordson tractors had new bright blue companions. Little did I realise then that the farming communities were in the midst of a great exodus from the land. Little did I know that I would have only one magnificent year with the farm horses before the onward march of machinery would change country life forever!

To the north, the green and pleasant slopes of the county of East Lothian folded slowly towards the sea, in the south they rose gently towards the Lammermuir Hills. The farm of East Windygoul lay on the flat southern perimeter of the small mining town of Tranent. Much local farmland, since the Second World War, had been consumed in answer to the great social demand of, 'Hooses, hooses and mair hooses.' Only two hundred of Windygoul's black fertile acres now remained. The traditional grey sandstone walls and orange pantiled roofs gave shape to the stables, the cattle courts, the piggery, the hayshed and granary and were all inward facing;

thus, in winter, all the animals were sheltered from the cold blasts but also shared their own warmth.

Bobby

Bobby was a gentle, dapple-grey Irish draft cross Percheron gelding with wide intelligent eyes set within a finely sculpted head. He was rising sixteen years of age, as indeed was I. He stood at sixteen hands to his withers. He had a deeply set chest, well-sprung ribs and neatly rounded hips, all set upon clean legs and small feet.

Our partnership began in bewildering fashion. I walked into his stall that first morning to be met with his two flashing rear hooves. When fitting his collar he sought to sink his teeth into my shoulder. Enough was enough for any man. In fear and in anger I snatched his upper lip, twisting it till he arched his back in cringing pain.

Raising my fist to his face, spluttering through clenched teeth I said:

'Do that to me again and you're a f*****g goner, son!'

His ears went horizontal with hurt. Slowly I eased my grip. His ears pricked forward. His head dropped. His nose muzzled into my dungarees. He was sorry. I was sorry. Putting my arm around his neck I whispered.

'Bobby, this isn't you, it isn't me! Bobby. This is not us my bonnie laddie!'

In that moment of tenderness I felt an awful rage well within me. Bobby's mane was laden with lice. His buttocks had been repeatedly pricked with the sharp steel tines of a hayfork. His hips were blistered like a field of molehills. The horse was demented; his temper was little short of breaking. Tied up in his stall he was completely cornered. In petrified anguish his only defence was to lash out with his rear hooves.

For four days and nights I resorted to shampooing, creaming and powdering. This brought peace to his body and soul. His head lifted, eyes shone, temper settled and his gait steadied. In time, his mane grew in, his tail filled out and his good looks and open heart returned!

I was to find out later of another wicked deed to which Bobby had been subjected. When yoked in the box-cart, his driver had pricked his hips with a darning needle. Bobby would rear up at the front and then clatter the bottom of the cart with his hind feet, bruising his hochs in his desperate flight from torture. To have witnessed, as I had, this hitherto mild and diligent horse become a tormented beast would have made any decent man weep, not to say a simple, growing country laddie.

On every Scottish farm there was a clearly defined pecking order of authority. The farmer would discuss the day's work with the farm grieve who would give the orders for the day to the foreman who drove the first pair of horses. In turn, he advised the other horsemen who drove the second, third, or fourth pairs of horses and so on down the stable until he came to the Odd Laddie who did odd the jobs with the odd or single horse, which, by tradition, was stabled in the bottom stall of the stable. (That was Bobby and I.) It was the foreman who kept the key to the medicine chest and the corn kist. It was he who rang the bell signalling the start of the day.

On that tinkle, all the harnessed horses slowly reversed from their stalls like clockwork toys and headed for the door. They found comfort in this routine. The horses assembled in the same ranks at the watering trough then held their respective positions as they marched, perhaps four pairs in a row, to a particular field. Even here, such as in a day's ploughing, the four pairs were yoked to their ploughs but moved off only on a signal from the foreman. This ritual was repeated in reverse at lunchtime and also when they loused at the end of their working day.

It was of course the foreman who built the first corn stack at harvest time, led with his first pair when carting, set out the red and white feering poles in the field to ensure straight ploughing, led the squad when singling the turnips and sugar beet, sowed the corn seed in springtime and instructed work to cease when the job became untenable due to heavy rain. I had the privilege of learning from three foremen: Duncan Jack at East Windygoul and Harry

Henderson and Jake Hogg at the neighbouring farm of the Myles.

Duncan was a tall silent man with deep brown, thoughtful eyes. Harry, a decade younger was genial and perceptive. Jake was the philosopher. All were highly intelligent and excelled in the daily craftsmanship of the farm. It was in their horsemanship that they truly displayed their 'touch of the master's hand.' They read each young horse. They understood their fears and calmed them. They didn't ribb, batter or abuse them. They didn't resort to devious trickery or brutality. They spoke to their young horses. They won their confidence and, in so doing, set up these young animals for life as dependable beasts. They were all Scottish horse-whisperers. Men like these could have, strolled through any university with ease. Such was the substance of the Scottish farm-worker of that period. They were creative, artistic, artisans.

The array of jobs that Bobby and I were called upon to do was dictated by the season of the year. Some jobs were fascinating, a few nauseating, many repetitive but none disinteresting. In spring we carted mangolds for the dairy cows and hay bales to the grazing fields of following heifers. After assisting the shepherd with the slaughter and skinning of the few hoggs that lay dying at the hedge backs, Bobby and I would cart the carcasses away and toss them down an airshaft which, at one time, had provided air to the miners working coal seams beneath our fields but at a great distance from the pit bottom. Perhaps the most frightening job of all was when we had the task of emptying the cottagers' ash tip. Whilst I was digging, rats would shoot out across my forearm or skiff across my shoulder.

We trimmed the turnip drills for singling with the scarifier in early summer. It was then too that we took the drum-shaped Pudding Cart which was full of rancid offal, discarded by the Co-op butcher shops and fleshing department, to the rat-infested municipal tip. The stench of the vile contents would literally have killed a horse but it was a nutritious change of diet for the vermin! No more attractive was when we were sent to empty the farm cottage cesspools. The smell in the high heat of summer did nothing if it didn't induce acute pangs of hunger in a growing lad.

Perhaps the most repetitive task of all was the hay pole. The farm workers stored the loose hay for use in winter by building it into large haystacks in the farmyard. They erected a thirty-foot pole, the pulley ropes of which were attached to a two-pronged fork; this was thrust into the hayricks which had been carted in from the fields. Bobby was yoked to the ropes and on stepping forward he raised the load of hay to the required height. The stackers would trip the fork, landing the hay precisely where needed. I would then reverse Bobby back a few paces to the starting line. For two long weeks we stepped slowly forward and slowly backwards. The only saving grace from that job was to finally see six massive haystacks built in beautiful symmetry.

Before the corn harvest, Bobby had frequent days of well deserved rest when I joined the other workers to single the turnips. Thereafter, I had spells with them stooking the sheaves in the corn fields. If the sheep had to dipped, clipped or moved to fresh fields, I would assist the shepherd.

Every job, in that first year of working life was a new experience. The shepherd once threw me his knife and instructed me to topple a dying sheep by thrusting his knife through its throat with a twist and hold it down until it kicked its last. In the piggery the pig-man threw young male piglets at me. I caught them in mid-air and held them upside down by the hind trotters. With two quick flicks of his razor blade they were castrated. I then disinfected their wounds with two quick squirts of pure Dettol from an oil pourrie.

Part of the autumn was spent in the potato fields. The tractor would spin the potatoes from the drills with the rotating digger; the potato pickers lifted them along the length of their stent. Bobby and I would then rake that ground with a single harrow to uncover those potatoes which had been trampled underfoot. It was at that time we saw the first signs of frost, which heralded the winter.

The cattle courts were then stocked with fattening bullocks, which Bobby and I had to bed on the Saturday mornings. The courts had low pantiled roofs supported by cast iron pillars in an odd assortment of places. To manoeuvre a long cart laden with straw in and around these bullock-filled courts demanded a skill, from Bobby, comparable to low-loader lorry drivers in the narrow streets of our historic cities.

With winter came the snow. The pairs of horses were confined to the stable when the land was frozen. There was no such respite for Bobby. We fitted sharp studs to his shoes which bit into the ice and helped Bobby from slipping on the treacherous roadways. We were, at times such as these, the only lifeline which kept all the farm animals fed. I took Bobby from Muirpark farm along Lover's Lane towards the Winton village road with a cart load of hay bales. At the junction, I turned him into the Balderstrip field, but as I nudged him and the long-cart through the gate the young heifers stampeded towards us desperate for a bite. Intent on keeping them in the field I walked backwards as Bobby shuffled forwards. As the cows surrounded us Bobby accidentally laid both his front feet on top of mine. I flopped backwards and as I lay anchored to the frosted field the cows saw me as a tasty bit too. With their long course tongues they licked at my beret, chewed at my hair, shaved my face, undid my jacket, pulled up my shirt and sucked at my vest. Bobby stood stock still looking down upon me. As I peered up his nostrils I could read thoughts.

'You stupid boy!'

I froze then prayed then bawled. Bobby, in time, lifted one hoof then the other and I was free to spread the hay.

After a few days of enforced rest the other horses became fresh; their sheaths and rear hochs would swell and their heels became itchy. The solution was in my hands.

When I was finished with the early trip round the fields to feed the stock I quickly stabled Bobby then took the other four horses, one at a time, out into the snow-covered fields. Fitted only with a bridle and short rein I mounted them bareback and would egg them on into a gallop. With my knees implanted in their withers they would romp around the field until each of the horses, Billy, Jock, Wull and Sandy, had had enough. Riding a one ton, six foot high Clydesdale horse at full gallop was as smooth as a carousel at a fair.

There were of course lighthearted moments whilst working with Bobby. In the late spring, his white coat turned to a deep dappled grey. I had fitted him with an open bridle which, set off with royal blue rosettes, gave a rather regal touch to his finely cast head. Riding bareback through town on this stylish steed I was subjected to calls of Wee Napoleon and Lord Godiva from the townsfolk.

In that scorching June of 1955, Bobby and I were at the haymaking. The sun was high, the work heavy, the hours long and I a growing lad. At three-thirty in the afternoon we stopped for our break. I took Bobby to the shady side of the hayricks where I sat down to have my snack. Two hours later I woke to find Bobby had gone. The wise old horse had gone no further than the other side of the rick. He had followed the shade. Going home that evening, apart from a smiling rebuke from the farm grieve, I felt it had been a good day. I had spent two hours dreaming of Ingrid Bergman— and got paid for it!

That was not my first aberration. There were five farms in the group between which Bobby and I regularly plied. After lunch one day we were taking a long-cart down the narrow road to Kingslaw farm, I was lulled by Bobby's rhythmic walk. Luckily, I didn't fall off the cart and under its wheel. Rather, I fell backwards into the cart and slept an unstoppable sleep. Bobby plodded on. Suddenly all Hell was let loose. I started from my sleep to the thunderous noise of shattering glass and the blasphemy of Willie Colquhoun, the travelling Co-op butcher. The poor man was pinned to the back of his driver's seat by our cart shaft, which had crashed, through the windscreen of his van. One cannot imagine the fear in his heart when he saw this driverless horse descend upon him. I've no doubt that he prayed. He certainly swore! Willie kindly told his boss that a passing Field Marshall tractor pulling a threshing mill and baler had thrown up a muckle stone which broke his windscreen.

At the potato planting in the spring, all the resources of the farm were thrown into one field. It was mesmeric to watch man, machine and horse so synchronised. Once the tilth was worked and the drills drawn Bobby and I preceded the potato planters with our cart loaded with the seed potatoes which we poured out into their hessian brats.

The ladies of the land were mainly middle-aged and ever ready to offer their best advice to a callow stripling such as me. One of my enjoyable little ploys was to quietly whistle a well-loved tune. The choir of angels never failed to respond. With Mima Kerr, Annie Cross and Jenny Wilson the sopranos, Meg Jack and Bessie Bathgate and Kate Clapperton the falsettos and Margaret Riley and Mary Ross the mezzo sopranos, all sang in perfect unison. The gentle tones and spirit of their sweet voices wafted across the tattie drills.

They sang the classic hymns, Abide with Me and All in an April Evening. They gave vent too to the then popular Rock 'n Roll Waltz and warmed to A Nightingale Sang in Berkeley Square and all without missing one seed potato!

The horsemanship in that potato field was of the finest. The real skill of the horseman, especially when splitting the drills so as to cover the seed potatoes, was in the method by which he tied his two horses together thus ensuring that they tread along the pinnacle of the drills without damaging the seed potatoes below. It was rewarding to watch these Clydesdales, Percherons and Suffolk Punch horses with their harness shining and buckles glinting, necks arched and every sinew pulling with confidence, intelligence and gentle obedience and their every step carefully measured: with power and style they secured that future crop. They were then, but alas no more, the bedrock of Scotland's productive economy.

One day the farm steward sent Bobby and I on the long trip to the coal depot at Tynemount. It was a pleasant afternoon, the sky was clear and the Lammermuir hills, by late August were aglow with the purple hue of the heather. That day the countryside seemed quieter, the birds screeched louder, the grass was greener, the trees stood taller, the miles seemed longer. Absorbing that breathtaking panorama from the height of the box cart, it seemed a perfect day. By nightfall, it would be for Bobby and me, a day not readily forgotten.

On reaching the coal depot I reversed the cart into the door of a sixteen-ton steel wagon. For the next hour it was heads down, tails up, shovel swinging. Suddenly I knew something was adrift. As the shunting engine passed it belched out black smoke and hissed white steam. Bobby had taken fright and shot off down the railway line.

I whispered to him then teased him and the cart back across a few rails until we were clear of them then I reversed him into the coal wagon. With twenty-five hundredweights of coal in the cart we set off for home.

Travelling through the tree-lined avenue of Ormiston village, I sensed a change in sound again but did not know from what. Leaping from the cart, I discovered that the pin holding the nearside wheel had fallen out. Wisdom had it that cartwheels were so designed that only if reversed would the wheel run off the axle. I borrowed a piece of fence wire and formed a makeshift pin which held until we arrived home late at East Windygoul farm.

Carter McNeill, the pig man, begged me to reverse the horse up into the main piggery building where the coal could be tipped out. This would save him barrowing it in. The row of piggery buildings were parallel to the farm track but were set at a lower level. I put Bobby at right angles to the piggery door which lay down a short decline and from where the piggery floor rose up a short, steep incline. This wasn't going to be easy on the horse. I whispered to Bobby and told him what I expected of him. With that, I grabbed his bridle and thrust him backwards down the slope. He poured all his honest might into the task. His front legs were straining at forty-five degrees His hind legs, with sparks flying from his shoes, were level with the ground. Yet the cart stuck firm! I hauled him back up the incline and then thrust him back down again, but at an angle, in the hope we could at least get the nearside wheel into the building then immediately swing him to the left and get both wheels in. Despite his grunts and snorts the cart refused to budge. Again we scrambled up the bank. By now Bobby was hot, agitated, lathered and pretty well spent. I had a quiet word with him and, once he had gathered his breath, we charged backwards in a final attempt. He pushed with all he had. His tail was brushing the ground when suddenly his leather bellyband snapped!

The weight of the coal swung the cart shafts up into the air yanking Bobby up with them. He was hanging by his collar with his feet flailing in mid-air. I, too, was up in the air with one hand clutching his bridle and the other clinging to his hames.

In a second the pig man smashed the back door of the cart with a large hammer. The coal fell out. The horse came down. I came down. The cart came down but with one shaft lying over his back and shoulders. Bobby took off in a blind gallop. Still holding onto his bridle and hames I was being dragged backwards as Bobby was trampled my feet with his clattering hooves. I swung my feet crises-cross around his knee. With every stride his great knee dealt a sickening thud between my legs. The pain was so excruciating that my hold on the horse was slipping fast — and still he thundered on!

If I had let go he would have trodden over the top of me and the cart would have finished me off. Two hundred yards down the farm road I finally got him stopped. The temporary pin had sheared. One wheel was off the cart. One shaft lay along his back and the other down his side. His saddle was under his belly and his breeching around his hind feet. I tried to stand, but slumped semi-consciously at his feet. Bobby trembled from tip to toe as the lather dripped from his belly and sweat poured down the insides of his rear legs. The froth snorting from his mouth fell upon my head and down inside my shirt. By the time the pig man had cut Bobby from the cart I had gathered myself sufficiently to walk him back to the stable. As that old horse and this young laddie staggered home up the brae together we were, that evening, a pitiful sight.

I put Bobby in the loosebox to let him settle then walked home. On sitting down to tea, I raised my soup spoon; my arm began to shake uncontrollably; the spoon rattled between my teeth. Moments later I was violently sick. After a short rest I returned to the stable and a neighing welcome from Bobby. With buckets of warm water I shampooed him from head to foot. I then used a cheese barrel hoop to draw the surplus water from his coat. After giving him a respectable bucket of bruised oats, a few new potatoes and a handful of mint sweets, I left him to dry out.

In the cool of the evening I returned to the farm. Bobby nickered. I opened the loosebox and stable doors, called on him and we made our way down the half-mile to the grass field where, with the other horses, he spent the summer nights. Leaving the stable without a halter as we always did, he pranced behind me giving me a playful nudge. I leapt upon his back then spun myself completely around and lay with my head on his neck and my feet along his hips as he meandered towards the field.

He had recovered from the earlier shock and felt refreshed after his wash. His grey dappled summer coat was clean and shining. Turning him out into the field, Bobby gave a gleeful little fling, bent his knees and proceeded to roll over and over on his back with all fours punching the sky. Then, with a quick shoogle, he dusted the stoor from his coat and galloped off, tail whisking, mane flowing, to join the other horses.

Next morning I waited in the stable with trepidation. The steward approached. I was convinced my end was nigh. But, to my complete surprise, Geordie Smith, a stout man with a glowering but cherubic face, put his arm across my shoulder and said,

'Well, Arthur, son, you did right to hold on to the horse.'

Greatly relieved, in those few seconds I grew ten feet tall. He then gave me a gift of a new rope bellyband which, as an old sailor, he had spliced and bound with pride. That day began a friendship, which was to last to the end of his life.

In the autumn of 1955, the second pair of horses, Sandy and Wull was sold at Lanark horse market. In the spring of 1956, the first pair, Billy and Jock was also sold. That left only Bobby. It became evident to me that it was only a matter of months before Bobby would go as well and, in truth, I felt that my attraction to the farm had always been the horses and thus I did not relish the prospect of life on a soulless tractor.

That autumn, a cattle float emerged slowly from the farm. I spotted Bobby's head swaying frantically out of the top. His neighing, his helpless pleading, as the lorry approached was heart-rending. I whistled and called out, 'Bobby! Bobby!' He swung his head round and nickered. The lorry slowly trundled over the hill and disappeared from sight. It was on its way to the slaughterhouse. I was mortified! I loved him but I could not save him. That was the last time I saw Bobby.

I knew that within an hour and a half, Bobby, who had given his all in this life, would be winging his way to that great stable in the sky. Perhaps he did meet again with his other memorable contemporaries — Wull and Sandy, Hector and Victor, Sandy and Star, Prince and Paddy, Donald and Clyde, Jean and Mary, all of whom, with great credit, had ploughed old Scotland's lands.

Perhaps, too, the good Lord may reserve a place for me as their groom. It will be a noble eternity.

The Red Cross Horse Parade

Arthur and Clyde

See that picture on the wa'

May oor guid God never let it fa'

For in that picture you can see

Twa braw lads: Clyde and me.

Clyde, he is a cheery horse

A gentle black grey gelding

He ploughed the knowe o' Birsley brae

And carted corn for threshing

But noo auld Clyde's getting din
His legs are stiff, his belly thin.
When first to the Myles he came
He wis neither lazy nor was he lame.

T'was whiskered Jock, the devil
That drove him on ower the stibble
And kept him oot in a' the rain
As though he was a muckle stane

But, yince tae Linton did we gone
His harness dazzled, his buckles shone
He took the Bowe Cup, a victory clear!
For Clyde and me 'twas a memorable year

(Arthur Greenan, aged thirteen years, 1953)

The Horse Whisperers
Photo by Kate Stephen,

Tommy Tempest and Bertram Buglass were life long chums who started work together as young ploughmen on a farm outside West Linton at the end of the last war. As boys they had skipped school, raided orchards, stole turnips from the farmer's field to make candle lit lanterns and had mumps together. In the winter evenings as they helped the horsemen to clean their harness; they listened to the epic tales of heroic horsemanship and learned the bothy ballads which the men sung as they beetled the leather, buffed the brasses and bagged the chains. As teenagers they shared bonds and secrets that would tie them together for all time. In their third year at the senior school they were teased in the playground by Mary, a tall girl with thin legs, tight curly hair and an impish smile, and her pal Marlene who was broadly set with a large face, heavy auburn curls and sensuous rubber lips. Mary twinkled with mischievous sex appeal whilst Marlene looked succulent.

The bold boys invited the two young ladies to visit them in their bivouac tent which they had pitched, out of sight of their parents, in a dip in the Station Hollow. That sunny Saturday afternoon, to the cheering in the distance of the visiting supporters of Ormiston Primrose football team, the four youngsters lunged at each other. In those explosive, reckless moments they all took each other to new horizons. Not a word broke the rhythm of their day.

Their kinship was anchored too by their ability to have a conversation with each other without speaking. Their communication was a nod, a wink, a glance, a shrug. It was a secretive code that they used in the presence of all third parties not least the local parish minister, the Reverend Ralph Bonkle.

Mr Bonkle rattled his knuckles on the door of the bothy in which they lived. Tommy Tempest peered out into the darkness.

'Ah! Come in Mr Bonkle. Please come away in and have a seat on that blanket kist. It's quick dark at night now, eh?'

'It is indeed Tommy. And how are you Bertram. Had a hectic day?'

'It was no bad at all, minister. Tommy and I have been busy breaking in a three year old filly to the plough. Luckily we've got a steady old mare to yoke her with so it went quite well.'

Such was the deceptive camouflage that horse whisperers used. Fifty years later Tommy recalled those two horses, Mary and Jean. Yes, the old mare was essential in introducing a young horse to heavy work but so too were his taming oils and herbs he used to steady the young filly. Tommy's preferred concoction, he told me, was aniseed, cinnamon, and nutmeg, tincture of opium, rosemary, and thyme. It worked with the young girls too, he asserted with a smile!

'Tommy, could ye put the kettle on and give the minister a cup of tea?' Bertram shouted through.

That evening the lads had stabled the horses with some haste and sprinted down the track to their bothy. It was Tommy's week to make their tea. As he peeled a handful of King Edward tatties in the sink Bertram lit the fire and boiled a kettle of water for the two to have a shave. They were intent on getting into Silverburn village hall to hear Jimmy Shand demonstrate a new Marino accordion which he had brought, strapped to his back, on his motor bike, all the way from Mr Forbes' shop in Dundee. The clock was ticking and Mr Bonkle was enjoying the warmth of the log fire. The lads looked at each other and nodded. Tommy Tempest held up a blackened chip pan.

'Mr Bonkle we're having chips for our tea, would you like some?'

The reverend gentleman looked across at the solid white circle of lard in the frying pan which was dotted by hillocks of black mouse droppings and tiny footsteps.

'Tommy, it really is an incredibly kind offer by both you and Bertram. I would love to have stayed much longer in such good company but the lady of the manse has a choir practice and I really must dash. I'm just so sad to go lads!'

'Oh don't worry about these black spots minister' Tommy advised. 'They disappear every time I heat up the chip pan!'

Each of them was initiated, on their twenty first birthdays, into the ultra secret and supremely learned Society of Scottish Horsemen. The ethos of the society was *One for all and all for One*. This was applied rigorously to the welfare of horseman and horse.

Bertram excelled at training Clydesdale horses for the farm and as reliable carters for the city of Edinburgh and the docks of Leith. Tommy, inspired by the ostlers in a travelling circus, also taught his horses a few extra performing tricks. All reacted instantly to the whispered commands of Tommy and Bertram in whom the horses had absolute faith. Both men could freeze any horse to the spot albeit those horses were ploughing with another person half a mile away. Both men too, could, on a whisper, persuade any horse to follow them through hoops of fire. With only a single rope they could lay a one ton Clydesdale horse out flat, and all without torture. Such was the trust of the horse in the skill of the whisperer.

They were sought out by the singing American cowboy, Roy Rogers, on his visit to Edinburgh's Empire theatre with his horse, Trigger. The national press clamoured for memorable photos. Unnoticed by the world, Tommy and Bertram, dressed as hotel porters, stood to attention at the foot of the grand stairway of the Caledonian hotel. Roy Rogers, mounted on Trigger who was a magnificent chestnut stallion with a flaxen mane and tail, approached the first step. The two porters turned and gently ascended the stair followed, obediently, by Trigger, to the tumultuous applause of the press. The portraits of Roy and Trigger in the upstairs bedroom were wired around the world. Trigger, like many a country lass, had found the odourless concoction of drawing oils, herbs of cinnamon, fennel, origanum and rosemary, which the lads applied secretly to their hands, irresistible.

Life, back on the farm was simple, hard and predictable. Their farm cottage, which had slits between the bare floor boards and slots between the roof pan tiles, was their bothy, their home. It was furnished with two single straw beds, one table, two chairs, a couple of kists for their clothes, a handful of pots and pans, assorted plates and bent spoons. As autumn turned into winter the ploughing months arrived. It was repetitive but precise. It had to be. The shallow, pointed, furrows turned over by the plough mould sat up like the teeth of a joiner's saw. It was into these serrations that the corn seed would fall in the Spring when broadcast by the swishing arms and flicking writs of Tommy and Bertram.

One Sunday evening they walked three miles to the Gordon Arms for a pint of heavy beer before parting to meet their sweethearts. As they quietly supped their ale the saloon door burst open and in skipped a clutch of strapping young lassies. They were all milk recorder students attending a three day course on surrounding farms. Both men turned away from the girls and swiftly anointed their foreheads with a hint of their drawing oils. Within twenty minutes it worked! Fair-haired Nell and Tommy skipped out into the garden shed whilst Jessie made good with Bertram in the hotel stable. Suitably fettled, these two girls slipped back unnoticed into the riotous melee When the men returned to the lounge bar, Daisy, a girl from Wigtownshire who had felt cut out by the other girls, thrust herself at Bertram who tiptoed her across the cobbles into the stable loft. Meanwhile Tommy Tempest headed for the railway station to meet Ruth, his girlfriend.

The chalk notice board told him that the last train from Edinburgh to West Linton was delayed. Tommy knocked on the door of Ruth's house and was welcomed in by her mother. Agnes had long black lustrous hair, a sallow complexion and the high cheekbones of her Romany forbears. She was a neat, divorced woman in her early forties with a firm, mesmerising bosom and beautifully delineated lips. Unknown to Ruth, Agnes, had for some time shared the thrill of Tommy's touch. This night, Agnes intended taking him to greater depths. Tommy aroused beyond revolt, banished morality from his mind. He knew that with black haired Agnes there was no going back. He tore at her clothes and then clawed at her body sinking his lips into the side of her neck. Just as she had intended!

Bertram arrived late at the cottage where Davina Copperstone, his fiancée, lived. She was in the huff. He had not been late before. There, in front of her family she subjected Bertram to a most terrible onslaught. This had not happened before either. Bertram steadied his nerve. He had arrived blindly intent on getting his body inside her dress but now aborted that plan. He strode out of her house in silent rage and walked home in the darkness to his bothy.

The next morning both men were in the stable at 5.30 a.m. In silence, the young rakes mucked out, fed, groomed and watered their pairs of Clydesdale horses then into the farmhouse kitchen, still in silence, for their porridge. Though physically tender and hung over they were sexually sated. They shuffled back to the stable in silence to harness their horses for a day's heavy ploughing but, by nightfall, the lads were out on the razzle yet again.

That night Bertram was invited into the house by Lizzie, Davina's stone-faced mother.

'Can I have a word with Davina?' He asked her.

'All in good time, young man.' Lizzie retorted.

'Why?'

'For the simple reason she that she is pregnant by you. So it is decision time, boy! What do you, as the father of this child, intend to do about her? You are also aware that unless you act quickly we will be the talk of the parish. So when will the wedding be, Bertram? Answer me! '

'Well, well, I wasn't really thinking of getting married, at least not for a while.' blurted Bertram. 'I mean, I widnae desert her, like. I'll happily pay for the upkeep o' the bairn.'

Pulling a turnip sheuk from under her pinafore the redoubtable Lizzie Copperstone pressed the sharp curved blade tight into Bertram's jugular vein.

Bertram wed Davina and they set up house in a cottage at her father's farm of Buckled Braes which was the neighbouring place to Tommy and Ruth, at Mount Myrtle. Tommy was successful at many agricultural shows with his Clydesdale horses in the best groomed horse, best cleaned harness and best decorated harness classes. Bertram was ever in demand in the spring and summer months by major breeders to travel around the highways and byways of Scotland with their premium stallions to meet around ten different mares each weekday.

Bertram Buglass, in time, became the new laird of Copperstone estate and Tommy Tempest was hired as his new farm manager. Then and forever they remained inseparable.

Their inordinate skills of horsemanship together with the secrecy and deception of the *Horseman's Word,* died with them.

St Peter's Stable

This poem tells of Bobby, the old dappled grey horse, whom I  drove on the farm in 1955, fifty-two years ago. I was but fifteen years old as indeed, was he. A year later a lorry appeared and Bobby disappeared forever. I missed him all those years then, one day in March, 2003, near the village of Earlstown, on the northern windswept coastline of Aberdeenshire, I stumbled upon Jenny, (*above*) a 20-month old, flaxen haired, Welsh cob Irish draft filly. She had Bobby's regal head. Some things are just meant to be...B

St Peter's Stable

A rickety lorry trundled

A nickering horse did cry

In two short hours a' coming

A life would surely die

Sprang open then, a golden gate
Stood noble, Jean and Clyde
In cantered old grey Bobby
Saint Peter by their side

A lonely lad stood waiting
A space descends his heart
On the windswept moor, she did appear
A sculpted work of art

His mind and soul were lifted
Forty years had passed
A flaxen welsh cob filly
His life returned at last

Yet still that man stood hoping
Will Bobby return to me?
'My man' said Pete
'I need a groom for all Eternity!'

The Acorn and the Oak

It was a frosty, starlit November night. Wee Mickey Smith was about to finish hawking vegetables around the doors of Muirpark Terrace in Tranent with his horse and cart. He aroused the suspicions of Sergeant John Costerton who decided to investigate.

Wee Mickey was half the height of his black Clydesdale horse, Bess. For decades he had hired himself, together with his horse and cart, to anyone in need of their services.

Black Bess

He would flit the families from the insanitary rows of miner's houses to newly built council houses, cart the slag from the railway station, and yoke the hay rake at East Windygoul farm. This quiet wee man, who was blind in his left eye, was well-liked for his readiness to help anyone. Three candles lit up Mickey's cart, one glass lantern at the front, one at the back and the third shone down upon the vegetables.

Sergeant John Costerton had been quietly demoted from Inspector then transferred to the countryside from the City of Edinburgh Police H Q , then in the town's High Street. His first slip was to turn out to guard the Queen, mounted on his police horse McBride. As Her Majesty rattled up the cobbles of Royal Mile in her coach, pulled by four greys, his horse, McBride, was drunk and so was he. But then to have been caught with Helen, a lady constable visiting from Glasgow City Police, in the tack room cupboard was the real cause of his downfall. Sergeant Costerton was determined to rebuild his reputation. He pounced on Mickey, pressing his torch into the wee hawker's face.

'And who are you, Sir?'

'God, you're bound tae know me. I'm Mickey Smith. Born and bred in Tranent. I've been here all my days, fifty-five years, anyway.'

'And where did these vegetables come from?'

'I grew them from seed. Just dug them oot o' my allotment this morning,' said Mickey, squinting up at Costerton with his good eye.

'And how did you come to possess this horse?'

'Oh, I've had Bess since I bred her as a foal.'

'Is that so, Mr Smith? Tell me then, how did you fall into the ownership of this cart?'

'Son' Mickey rasped, 'I've had it since it wis a bloody wheelbarrow!'

Star Looks Down

Arthur and Star

The sadness at leaving behind my primary school chums in July 1952 at St Martin's to head for Holy Cross Academy in Edinburgh lifted when I arrived at Kings Law Farm. The farm workers had returned from their five-day annual holiday and good weather had given them an early start to the hay-making.

The long grass had been cut earlier by a two–horse reaper and left to dry in the warm breeze under a cloudless sky. Shortly after, it was hand turned into small huts and left to make for a further week. Using a Tumbling Tam, a horseman swept ten of these kyles together which were then hand forked by the women farm workers into seven-foot high ricks, each around a ton in weight.

A small convoy of horsemen, each with a low sloping horse-drawn bogey, carted the ricks into the stack-yard. A huge grappling fork was then thrust into the rick. The hay was raised up a thirty-foot pole which swivelled to deposit its great load precisely where required on the massive haystack which the farm workers were building.

As a twelve-year-old then, I was mesmerised with the synchronised ebb and flow of this highly skilful operation. It was then that Star, a pure black Clydesdale horse, meandered into the stack-yard on his own. Star was seventeen hands to his withers, with four white legs and a *ringle'ee* - a luminescent halo around his left iris. His fine black head was enhanced by a tiny white star-like splash on his forehead.

The farm steward, Geordie Smith, beckoned to me.

'Come here, Arthur. If I give you a leg up do you think you could take the horse back tae Stan? He and Joy are down the bottom of the Muir hay field.'

'Oh. Aye, Mr. Smith.' I replied, eager to please.

'With us taking time to shift the big pole to make a new haystack, Stan, I imagine, will have dozed off. On ye go, son, the horse is canny enough.'

Mounted on this sturdy steed I turned out onto the road. At once I felt an overwhelming sense of power! I was struck by the magnificent views of the Fife coast which I saw for the first time from such a height.

'Come back Roy Rogers.' I thought 'You and Trigger are forgiven.'

When I was sure that no one was around I sang 'A Four Legged Friend' strumming on my make believe guitar.

The two workers in the hay field were twenty-two-year-old Stan and Joy, a prim early-forties maiden, who prepared the ricks for carting and used the might of Star to pull them on to the hay-bogies.

Too soon, we turned into the Muir field. The second crop of hay had already grown to two feet high and running down through were the sentinel rows of hay ricks. As we sauntered to where I thought Stan and Joy would be, I spotted a beautiful white swan bobbing in the long grass. As we drew nearer I realised to my horror that it was not a swan at all. It was Stan's bare bum and its' wings were Joy's bare knees! They were oblivious to Star and me. I was shocked and embarrassed down to my uppers. Within a few feet of reaching them I slid off the horse and hid. I was mortified!

Star nudged forward and, bending down, he licked Stan's bare bum! Stan let out the most horrendous roar! Star breenged forward, trampled on Joy's foot and broke her ankle! Stan quickly gathered himself:

'Hurry, son, round the other side of Joy and give me a hand.'

I had to comply.

'When I lift, you pull.' he instructed.

With eyes shut, I pulled up Joy's pale green bloomers. Next, it was up with her dungarees.

Stan, the quick witted survivor, turned menacingly to me:

'Take that and shut your face. Don't you dare tell a soul'

I pocketed his shilling in fear.

Never again did I experience feelings of such searing sympathy. Within a fleeting second Joy had plummeted from ecstasy to agony. To watch that poor woman, writhing and screaming with pain, as she was so ignominiously carted off, on a hay-bogey, to the doctor is forever etched in my memory. It was such an inglorious ending that had had such a celestially sensuous beginning.

Brother to the Ox

The book, 'The Brother to the Ox', written by Fred Kitchen in 1944 and reviewed in The Scotsman newspaper in July 2006 reminded me of the similar conditions of life and work suffered by the Irish field workers that I witnessed in East Lothian in the early 1970's. Had it appeared then, the The Scotsman would most probably have been blackballed too by many landowners in East Lothian. We most decidedly were!

The only sin I committed was to join with Father Michael Cassidy from Pathhead, and Father Michael Walsh from Dunbar, in seeking to end the brutality which pervaded many Irish potato picker's bothies in East Lothian. Worse still, East Lothian County Council officers had little knowledge of the existence of these bothies or the behaviour of the group of rogue Irish gaffers who used them.

Their workers were held, not in regulated farm bothies, but in dilapidated farm cottages dotted around East Lothian and Berwickshire. Girls slept in the same bedrooms as the young men. Pregnant girls like Margaret Macdonald, who lived in the Black Hut at Aberlady and worked on the land till the day she was due to give birth had been kicked up the backside, by her gaffer, in the last week of her pregnancy when it was found that she could not keep up with the speed of the potato digger. A week after giving birth in hospital she was bundled out of the squad onto the road and left to fend for herself. She had no money, no accommodation and help from no one. Elderly men too, were imprisoned, by having their clothing confiscated in freezing conditions, in a bothy with broken windows, near Humbie. Many were mentally sub-normal having been abducted off the streets of Edinburgh and Newton Aycliffe to replace the original Irish workers who had had fled from the grip of their brutal gaffers. All the workers lived in fear of their lives from the enforcers within each squad who meted out regular beatings in the fields and in the bothies. Some of the more able workers were spirited away through a system of safe houses which we had organised. They then made it back to Ireland.

All this was allowed to happen in East Lothian and Berwickshire. Many farmers knowingly used the services of these thugs. All three of our little team, Father Cassidy, Father

Walsh and me were subjected for months to an endless stream of abusive telephone calls, each one threatening to have us done in. In winter too they sought to lure the three of us out into dark country lanes for a chat.

Senior Labour councillors, who held committee convenerships-by grace of the majority of Tory county councillors- were not prepared to jeopardise their status in defence of *a bunch of Irish tinks*, as Labour leader, Councillor Dickie Wilson described them. Three major Tory landowners sought to have us silenced too. The Catholic Church in Ireland, classically, threw up their hands in mock horror when they learned what was happening to their parishioners abroad-only to claim Scotland was outwith their jurisdiction!

We needed the help of principled folk like Councillor Andrew Purves of Ormiston and Councillor Tommy Gunn of Prestonpans to bring an end to the dehumanising treatment of these immigrant workers through whom many in East Lothian, this, the garden of Scotland, had prospered. When all of the statutory authorities, whom John P Mackintosh, MP, had enlisted, were about to launch a surprise raid on these villains it was the Irish church, again, who panicked and blew their cover.

The County Sanitary Inspector who thought that his staff had examined all the official bothies in East Lothian did not realise that the bothies we guided him to were not the registered ones but despicable hovels hidden from sight within semi-derelict farm cottages.

I was then blasted by an elderly aristocrat, Lady Broun-Lindsay. As chairman of the Sanitary and Public Health Committee of East Lothian County Council she fiercely berated me for daring to criticise her Councillors and Officers in the local press. Their indolence in this matter had caused me to liken then to Rip van Winkle.

'Mr Greenan' she roared down the phone 'You are a working class upstart!'

I was rocked back on my heels by the ferocity of her attack. Once I had gathered my wits I realised that this poor woman knew nothing of this problem, so I hit her Achilles' heel.

'Lady Broun-Lindsay,' I pleaded, 'as a Catholic and as a Christian and as a human being I condemn the conduct of these gaffers. Now, my bonnie lassie, you're a Catholic and you're a Christian and you're a fellow human being, do you condemn these thugs?'

'Mr. Greenan, you are a most impertinent fellow, but I will resolve this matter tomorrow.' She asserted.

And she most certainly did.

The next morning, escorted by the police and with the support of Councillors Andrew Purves and Tommy Gunn, two men good and true, she bundled her bewildered committee members and timorous officers into a mini bus for a tour of inspection of every bothy in East Lothian. At the first bothy, outside Dunbar, she marched in, viewed the squalor and the filthy living conditions of the petrified workers and the clarty unclad children. Spinning around she strode out of that house and was immediately sick upon the grass verge. She dragged them through bothies in Tranent, Humbie, Aberlady, East Linton and Dunbar. By the end of the day she was finished. So too was the brutality of the Irish bothies. She saw to that!

In the aftermath, the County Sanitary Inspector sidled up to me and whispered angrily in my ear.

'Mr Greenan, I must say that with a bastard like you for a friend, who needs enemies?'

Decent Irish gaffers, like Pat Mills, who were known to treat their workers fairly, invited me to their homes for a cup of tea. They sent me on my way with a nice piece of smoked Irish bacon for my Sunday breakfast too.

The Dying Ploughman

'Ploughing' by Eirene Hunter

The wintry winds were blowing soft around my lonely stable loft
And, as the sun sinks in the skies, oh lay me down nae mair tae rise
Amid the sky light, dusky red, the sunbeams wander round ma bed
My time on earth has no been lang, my time has come and I must gang

It's only just a week this morn that I was full o' health and scorn
Full o' life and strength and fun as ony man among the throng

The doctor left in quite guid cheer but fine I kent that death was near
Something in ma briest gaed wrang, a vessel burst and blood oot-sprang

Farewell ma friends my neighbours kind, my weel kent face I hope you'll mind
Farewell ma plough for wi' these hands, I'll turn nae mair o' Scotland's lands
Farewell ma horse ma bonnie pair, I'll yoke an' louse wi' ye nae mair

I've served my maister weel and true, my weel done work he'll never rue
An' sairly on this earth I've striven, tae reach the golden gates o' Heaven!

Part Two

I had lived all my youthful life on the very southern outskirts of the town of Tranent. There was nothing, not even a telegraph pole, to impede my panoramic view of the Lammermuir hills eleven miles away, hence my spiritual attachment to the countryside. I went out of my mother's front door to the farm and out of her back door into the town for her messages. In the mid fifties, the onward march of mechanisation wrought the demise of the Clydesdale horse from the countryside forever. The loss of farm horses like Bobby, Tommy, Clyde and Pride was, for hundreds of people like me, a bereavement not easily forgotten.

All our neighbours were miners so it was suggested to me that I should now try the National Coal Board for work. I did so and became an electrical engineer but not before I had repaid the £2 loaned to me by Mrs Meg Jack and her husband Duncan. My mother was a young widow with eight children then and simply did not have the two pounds I needed for my bus fare which would enable me to start my apprenticeship.

Of the original stories, other than to have changed a name lest it caused any injury, I have retained all other aspects.

In the hustle and bustle of the coalmines I entered my second term at the University of Life.

The Miner's Story

It was lunchtime, January 1959. Three hungry apprentices, Joe Kilday and Ginger McCall and I each guzzled our piece. Matt Lynch the fair haired, jovial head store-man, whistled as he read his *Daily Express*. As a fellow whistler I turned to Matt.

'What is that tune, Matt?' I asked.

'That, my friend is *The Miner's Song*. You don't know it, Arthur?'

'I've never heard it before. No, Matt, I haven't.' Are you in fettle for a wee chant?' I asked him.

In the corner of that high barn, festooned with picks, shovels, wires and chains, we listened to the fullness of Matt's fine baritone voice as he sang these words:

The Miner's Song
Now I'd like you all to know, I'm a miner down below
Where there's ne'er a breath to cool the atmosphere
In the darkness and the damp, with my shovel and my lamp
 I've worked there, man and boy, these forty years

We're keeping the home fires burning and the big wheels turning

That's the job the miner has to do
Home and industry they depend on you and me
Pull together and we'll pull this country through

It's a tough life at the face and it takes a hardy race
For danger is there to meet you every day
We have our ups and downs in the smoky mining towns
When clouds are dark, I always smile and say

We're keeping the home fires burning and the big wheels turning
That's the job the miner has to do
Home and industry they depend on you and me
Pull together and we'll pull this country through

Now, when I was just a lad I got started with my dad
He used to teach me everything he knew
All the secrets of the mine. Man! it's just a battle time
But he taught me how to win those battles too

We're keeping the home fires burning and the big wheels turning
That's the job the miner has to do

Home and industry they depend on you and me
Pull together and we'll pull this country through

Around the fire at night when the coals are glowing bright
And the baby's there upon his granny's knee
There's a glow comes in my heart as I see the miner's part
In the fight to build the world that bairn will see

We're keeping the home fires burning and the big wheels turning
That's the job the miner has to do
Home and industry they depend on you and me
Pull together and we'll pull this country through

I had lost those hand-written notes which Matt had patiently dictated to me but then, forty five years later in the rafters of my house in East Linton, I found them. Matt Lynch's song is but a passing reminder of the life and times of all British miners, many of whom sought to improve their own working conditions and the lives of their fellow workers, not only through parliament, but at the coalmines too.

The death knell tolled for the coal industry in Britain when the miners were lured, as reluctant pawns, onto the chessboard of two political megalomaniacs: Mrs Margaret Thatcher, Prime Minister of Great Britain and Mr Arthur Scargill, President of the National Union of Mineworkers.

It was heart rending in 1985, to witness the selfless work of these miners and that of their predecessors implode as Mr Scargill, their last leader, led them from behind into a battle they did not want and into a war they could not win. He harboured the personal ambitions of a field marshal; he lacked the foresight of a field mouse!

Mrs. Thatcher ensnared the miners onto her battlefield at a time of her choosing.

They were trodden into the ground by thundering hooves of police horses which were twice the size and twice the weight of any pit pony that any miner had ever yoked. They were brutally pummelled by the batons of the members of Her Majesty's Constabulary, that impartial instrument of State and defender of British democracy. In the coalfields of Ayrshire in Scotland and in Yorkshire and Derbyshire in

England, their horses showed more sensitivity to the miners in flight than the clod-hopping officers mounted upon them. Thus the Tory government destroyed the mining industry forever.

So, let the youngsters of tomorrow look back and ask themselves this:

Who were?'

Keir Hardie. Bob Smillie and Mick McGahey from Lanarkshire.

Nye Bevan from Wales.

Joe Gormley from Lancashire.

Abe Moffat from Fife

And what did they do?

All these men were fearless yet pragmatic union leaders. They sought to protect the miners of Britain throughout the 20th century. In one year alone, 160,000 miners were injured and 2000 killed. In another year, striking miners were starved back to the pits to work longer hours for less pay. In yet another year, 432,000 miners were made unemployed.

The National Union of Mineworkers grew out of the first ever area union to be formed in Britain which was that of East Lothian. It was created by men from the pits around the town of Tranent and the village of Ormiston, the birth places of Joe Kilday, Ginger McCall and I.

Around 1200 AD monks walked from Newbattle Abbey through the Parish of Tranent to the shore at Prestonpans to extract salt from the sea. As they rested on their homeward trek, one of them pulled a lump of black shiny material from the bank and threw it onto their fire. That piece of coal ignited giving birth to the coal industry and the Mineworkers Union as we came to know it.

Aye, if only those monks could see us now.

They would surely weep!

Pate's Kilt

Pate and Rab were packers down the pit. They built stone pillars to support the roof which kept the coalface open and the miners safe. The miners dug the coal out during the day. The packing was a night shift task. Pate and Rab had worked as mates together for fifteen years down the Fleets Colliery near Elphinstone.

Every summer, when the season of pipe band competitions was at its height Pate, as the Pipe Major of the Fleets Colliery Pipe Band, had responsibility for its performance. It was imperative that he be present each Saturday morning to conduct them in the piping competitions. On the Sunday evening his pipe band had been chosen to lead two thousand pipers in that Grand Finale of the most famous pipe band parade in the world, the Cowal Highland Games. Television cameras would present them to Elphinstone and to the world! Thus Pate was forever trying to juggle his pit work with his love of piping. As Friday night ticked into the small hours of Saturday morning Pate became more anxious. It was unthinkable that he should miss the bus and Scotland's greatest international piping contest of the year. Without him his band would be leaderless. They would surely disintegrate. By four in the morning their work was on target. It was then that Pate turned to his mate.

> 'Rab, could you nip up the pit, run down to our cottage and chap up my wife, Nessie, and ask her for my kilt and my piping gear? I'll stay on and finish the job.'

Pate could be up the pit for five o'clock and still have time to get washed, shaved and shifted into his kilt. The band bus was coming at six. He'd be off to Cowal to birl his troops into winning action like they had never been birled before!

Rab turned and ran to the pit bottom. He persuaded the colliery oversman and the banksman to allow him up the pit shaft to the surface. He hurriedly undressed, threw his working clothes into his dirty locker, had a quick shower then dived into his clean clothes. He raced down the rows of miners' cottages in the dark to Pate and Nessie's house.

Gasping for breath, Rab battered on their door. Nessie opened the door and peered out into the dark.

'What is it? What do ye want at this time of the morning?' She snarled.

'Pate's kilt! Woman, Pate's kilt!' wheezed Rab.

Nessie fainted!

Welsh Courage

He had seen it. He had done it.

And as that icy night unfurled he would earn the tee shirt too. But Taffy Williams didn't know what this Sunday nightshift in January, 1964, was to hold for him.

Monktonhall Colliery which was being developed as a totally new deep coal mine was the shape of rugby posts at three thousand feet high but sunk down into the earth instead. The cross bar represented the road linking the two shafts at fourteen hundred feet down their length. The uprights represented No 1 Downcast Shaft where the cold air was sucked down into the pit, and to No 2 Upcast Shaft, where the warm misty air was sucked up out of the pit. Each shaft had its own winding engine poised on top and a water pumping station at the bottom. Water trickled through the pressure release holes in the six-foot thick concrete walls into circular garlands. These overflowed and spewed the water to the pit bottom only for it to be pumped back up to the surface and piped down into the Firth of Forth. Two other factors colluded to ensure disaster that night. The massive fan on the top of the No 2 Upcast shaft sucked all the warm air out of the pit, and in doing so sucked freezing replacement air down No 1 shaft into the pit at ferocious speed. The second was the repair platform. The water, cascading down from the garlands, was forced across this platform and down through a six foot square hole in the middle of it where the steel guide ropes ushered the lightweight cage through on its way to the pit bottom.

Taffy Williams was the Oversman. He had total responsibility for the pit during this night shift. He had come into the Lamp Cabin with Peter and Jimmy, the two pump house attendants, to uplift their electric cap lamps and Davy safety lamp. I was standing-in for the night shift lamp cabin attendant.

> 'It's howling a gale out there, Taffy. The builder's crane is spinning and swaying out of control. What a way to spend a Sunday night!' said I.

> 'I know, Arthur,' said Taffy 'and it's twenty three degrees below freezing on the surface so God only

knows what the temperature of the air rocketing down the shaft will be tonight. Arthur, the wind chill would cut you in half. Anyway, I'd better get going, the pump attendants will be waiting for me at the pit head. Peter from Mayfield, he's at the fourteen hundred feet pumps and Jimmy from Tranent is doing the pit bottom pumps.'

'Taffy, see you in the morning. I'll have the kettle on for you.' I said.

The downcast shaft was not yet in production but it was the only way to reach the 1400 foot level and the pit bottom pumps. The cage in which they went up and down the shaft was a simple lightweight frame made in the pit workshops. It was only capable of carrying four men. These three men wore an abundance of clobber. Cap lamps, Davy lamps, waders, Mayflower hats, oilskin coats, tea flasks, valve keys, notebooks and *Lady Chatterley's Lover* camouflaged as *Pilgrim's Progress*.

Twenty minutes had barely gone when the night silence of the Lamp Cabin was broken by the shrill of the phone.

'Arthur, Arthur! Ye better get the manager there has been a mishap in the shaft. And be quick about it!'

I dug the manager out of bed. He instructed that all the emergency services be called out, which I did. Flashing lights, doctors, ambulances and police soon raced to Monktonhall Colliery.

As Taffy, Peter and Jimmy had descended down the pit, Ninian Wightman, the winding engineman could see from his big rotating control dial that the men were approaching the square hole in the temporary platform. He slowed the engine right down to take the cage safely through the hole in the platform.

Not so.

The cage was stuck fast!

What no one could see were the massive bollards of white ice that had formed on the cage guide ropes.

The lightweight cage with the three men inside had gently come to rest on these ice blocks which easily took their weight. Down the shaft the steel winding rope piled and piled and piled. The rope lashed into coils around the inside of the shaft skipping past a compressor on the platform and tumbling down around the men's ears with great ferocity.

The only light they had, in the horrendous noise and pitch black, was their cap lamps.

Taffy, in an act of sheer bravado, opened the cage door and bawled.

'When I shout jump, bhoy, you jump!'

Peter jumped. Jimmy jumped. Taffy jumped. All three were now standing near the centre of the repair platform and yet the steel winding rope whipped coils down around them. Taffy dragged the two men across the platform.

'When I tell you to jump again, you just jump. Go! Peter, jump! Jimmy, jump! Jump!'

Taffy watched the rope above and in an instant he too jumped. All three were now squashed behind the compressor and pinned to the wall but protected from the flailing rope. Five seconds later the ice bollards on the guide ropes cracked.

The horrific screech of the steel rope and the cage scraping through the square hole in the platform and plummeting down the shaft ceased.

All was deadly silent.

All were alive.

Peter and Jimmy looked at Taffy with a gaze fixed with fear.

'What next Taffy?'

'Aw, f**k it, lads' said Taffy 'let's have a cup of tea then we'll work out what to do next. At least we're still alive.'

Peter and Jimmy stepped forward, with a look but not a word, and shook Taffy by the hand.

Astonishingly, it was too early in the development of the shaft to have a sophisticated electronic system of signalling. Phones had not yet been installed. This danger had not been foreseen. The only form of communication with the surface was a primitive iron wagon buffer which ricocheted sound up the pit shaft when pelted with a steel bolt. The only way to retrieve these men was to pull them back up in the same battered little cage.

'Peter, give the winding engine man three bells,' Taffy instructed.

The cage was raised from the pit bottom. It stopped at the wooden platform. The three bedraggled men stepped in silence into the cage for the slow ascent to the surface and to safety. The ropes and the cage, though distorted, held. When they reached the pithead all three offered to go back to work. Peter was instructed by the doctor to be driven home. Jimmy was taken to hospital and detained for a day. Taffy came meandering into the Lamp Cabin.

'Taffy sit down, you're as white as a ghost. Here's a good strong coffee. I'll get you transport home.'
'Arthur, you will not. I'm not going home. It'll just upset the wife. I've been through worse than this when I was in the mines in South Africa.'

There was a loud clatter. I spun round to see Taffy's eyes lolling in their sockets. Taffy was on the floor. He was out for the count. His night's work had ended.

The Black and White Minstrel

We gathered at six thirty on Saturday morning in the electricity substation at Newcraighall Colliery. It was here that the main power lines came in from the high voltage electricity poles, down through large transformers and oil filled switches and out through separate cables to feed different parts of the colliery both on the surface and underground.

Willie Prescott and Jacky Smith were the tradesmen. Peter Clark and I were their respective apprentices. Our purpose was to cut out a number of 3300 volt cables which ran between Substation 1 and Substation 2. Once we had disconnected the power we had to pursue each section of the job to its completion before we could call it a day. Jacky Smith turned to me:

> 'Right, Greenan, you wee fart, you're the shortest of the lot of us so just get down into the cable duct and trace that cable to No 2 Substation. Then do exactly the same in reverse. Mark it both ways with this white chalk.'

'Jacky, that is definitely the cable. I've checked both it both ways. God, my knees are skinned with all this crawling.'

'Aw shut yer greeting face.' He smirked. 'Ye don't complain when Father Murphy makes ye kneel for two hours on bare boards in the chapel, do ye?'

'Willie that is the switch you need to isolate. The seventh from your right when you're standing round the back. Have you got that?' Jacky asked Prescott.

There were thirteen high voltage, oil filled switches in the row.

'It's OK Smithy. I know what I'm doing. I wasn't born yesterday.' Prescott rasped.

Jackie beckoned me. We moved out to work elsewhere. Prescott stank. He had not been to bed and was still pissed from his Friday night on the razzle.

Peter Clark worked for Willie Prescott.

'Clark, you useless prick, where are you?'

'Working, Willie! I'm behind you, Willie.'

'Right,' said Prescott 'Cut that cable there. That one there' he pointed. 'It is sixth from the right at the front.'

'Willie that just does not add up. It's the seventh cable from the right that I should cut.'

'Clark just do as I tell you or you'll be added up.'

'Willie, for God's sake listen to me. It's not the right one. It is definitely not the right one'

'Now just cut that cable, Clark.

'No, Willie I can't. Count it again and you'll see it's the wrong cable. Honestly!'

Prescott, who was a snide fellow when sober but was an absolutely evil sod with a drink, lunged at Peter and pressed his hacksaw blade to his throat.

'You've taken the piss long enough Clark. Cut that cable or you'll get this hacksaw across your f*****g throat and this screwdriver down your ear hole!'

Peter Clark, a competent, conscientious but gentle sort, relented. He started to saw through the 3300 volt cable. He cut through the outer earth wire. He cut through the greaseproof paper insulation. He sawed through the lead sheathing. Then he hit the 3300 volt live copper conductors.

The head bursting noise and the blinding blue flash filled the room with instant light and acrid smoke. They staggered around in the dark, disorientated and bewildered and not sure whether they were still alive or not. It was a violent out of body experience for them both. Willie Prescott spewed his guts up. Peter Clark coughed then froze. He looked like Al Jolson. Face black, eyes white, hands black, lips white, hair singed, eyebrows vanished. He looked like a black and white minstrel. Only the hacksaw handle was left in Peter's hand. The rest of it was blobs of molten metal stuck to the floor.

Peter Clark had cut through the outer earth sheath and into the live conductors. He had received a belt of 3300 volts. The high voltage oil filled switch had ignited then melted in flashes of blue smoky light.

'You stupid bastard!' bawled Prescott.
Prescott never knew what hit him. Jacky Smith, grabbed him by the scruff of the neck marched him off his feet and dumped him on the floor of the chief electrical engineers office.

'Jacky. Steady. Steady. What is going on?' The chief demanded.

Jacky Smith was raging.

'You take this clown Prescott and do what the blazes you want to. He's not working with us. He's still pissed from last night and nearly killed young Clark. And as for you, you're some flaming gaffer letting a galoot like that start work this morning anyway!'

The National Coal Board apprentices who attended Esk Valley College in 1960. in the back row, left to right are Roy Mooney, George Seigle and Arthur Greenan. Kneeling at the front are John Wilkie and Peter Clark.

The boss came round to the substation and gave Peter a pat on the head. It wasn't a fatality so it was O.K. No need to call in any outside officials about this. It could be handled quietly. Peter was given a cup of tea.

> 'You're O.K then to carry on for the rest of your shift Peter? That's a good lad now, just a simple error.' He asserted as he slunk from the sub-station.

Willie Prescott wasn't sacked. He was sent home to sleep of the drink.
Nothing further was heard of the matter.
So it was in 1962.

Dod Scott, the Miner

Why should Dod Scott go to Hell?

I first saw him was when, as a child, I was invited by Dod and his wife Mary to their street party in the wee roundel of council houses known as Muirpark Terrace at the close of the Second War. Every neighbour, with their children, was herded onto the green within the small circle houses which had been our homes and refuge for the five years in which war had raged in Europe. Bombs had dropped near Winton and Macmerry, but a mile from our homes.

Dod, a coalminer, was lean, broad and quiet. He left the organizing of his life to his wife, Mary, who was a matronly, ruddy faced woman from Lewis in the Outer Hebrides, hence her charming nomme de plume of Highland Mary.

The party was a farewell fling for their daughter Rachael and her friend, Regina, of whom it was whispered that they had spent much of the war operating secret signalling systems.

The two girls had met their future husbands whilst in the services who, by coincidence, were both Australian. One came from Melbourne and the other from Alice Springs.

The fun, that warm evening in June, 1946, began with the older schoolgirls organizing games for the smaller children of whom I was one. We played all the cissie games: ring-a-ring-a roses, rounders, peevers and tig till our dads began to trickle home from work and swell the numbers. We were all given small cups of Irn Bru. The parents were invited into Dod's front garden which was enclosed in a high privet hedge. After a handshake and a hug they too were served up their Johnnie Walker whisky but camouflaged as 'Irn Bru'. The birling and the skirling, the hooching and the shooching, the flinging and the singing had risen to a crescendo as twilight fell. It was brought to a sudden hush with the arrival of a black Co-op taxi which purred to a halt at Dod and Mary's door.

Our parents and neighbours formed a chain of hands around the taxi and as the fiddler played they quietly sang:

Now is the hour when we must say goodbye
Soon I'll be sailing far across the sea

As the falsetto built these two tearful young ladies, garlanded by old friends and neighbours ran to the cab to be whisked off, forever, to start their new lives in distant new world called Australia.

The next time I saw Dod it was a dark winter's night.

'Arthur, take the wheel barrow over to Dod Scott's back door and make sure not a soul sees you.' That was dad's command.

It was a pitch black night. As a ten year old I was thrilled, excited, and changed gear into my commando mode. I hid in the shadows as a courting couple laughed and had a wee squeeze and a peck as they passed. I ducked down too when a policeman on his bicycle with the upright handlebars and a carbide lamp cycled past but I did get safely to Dod's back door.

'Hold that candle just there, son.' Dod ordered.

His big hands fumbled around inside our home made wheel barrow and, as if by magic, a wee bag of sugar appeared. I didn't know it was there. How did he?

'Is this for me? Is it from your Dad? Good lad.'

I just didn't know that two big grown ups colluded. I didn't know that my Dad had first call on all that came into the back shop of the Co-op grocery where he worked. Dod was paid seven tons of coal as part of his wages as mine driver at the Fleets Colliery. He lifted my barrow up to the top step, filled it with great lumps from his coalhouse and lowered it to the ground with ease. I was agog at the strength of this rough hewn man. And so Dod's coal kept my Dad and Mum and their seven bairns warm in the winter.

Dod, meanwhile, savoured the odd banana, which Dad had got him. It was a change from the usual Co-op cheese, and home made jam piece that Dod carried down the Fleets for his daily break.

Eight years later, as a young teenager, I was sitting in St Martin's chapel. My feet were freezing, my knees, hands and ears were freezing, my backside, which was stuck to the solid wooden pews, was freezing too.

That Sunday evening at Benediction, Father Murphy ranted as he laid into the lapsed Catholics who never showed face in his church. Then he attacked those Catholics who had married Protestants and left his church. He then warned the sparse congregation that if we did not attend Mass every Sunday in this a large, unheated, Dutch barn of a church our souls could not enter the Kingdom of Heaven. They would be blackened forever by mortal sin and that I, like those Presbyterians, would perish in Hell!'

I suddenly remembered that Dod Scott was a Presbyterian. I was mortified. Then I thought of Dod Scott going to Hell. Presbyterian or not he had risked his job by giving his neighbours, my Mum and Dad who were Catholics, a barrow load of concessionary coal on numerous occasions to warm them and their Catholic children. By what authority did Father Murphy speak? I asked myself. Was this suppression by design? Was it oppression by intent? Was this control-freakery at its most unchallenged?

It was a fear that was bred into the souls and minds of us, the biddable working class Catholics. It was burnt onto our brains that this was the will of God whose will we were not permitted to question.

No. It was not the will of God! It was the will of Father Murphy and his ilk who creamed a comfortable life off the back of my frightened, impoverished parents and their generation.

He never ever went hungry. Fear saw to that. Even the poorest parishioners were cajoled into putting on his plate the amount suggested by him. It was power without responsibility. It was fear of the most evil kind.

That seed of doubt was sown in my young mind fifty years ago, not about faiths, not about my *Higher Power*, but of man–made religious establishments. Father Murphy's man-made machine, his man-made church has imploded in sodomy throughout Europe, Australasia and America.

My faith in Dod Scott's decency did not!

His beacon burns in my mind to this day.

The Coming of the Light

Harry Burton, a small bluff Yorkshire man, was as bright as a button. He could explain the safety system on the winding engines at the new Monktonhall Colliery which consisted of dozens of limit and proximity switches with blinding clarity to any novice. An innovative engineer, Harry was, in 1963, our mischievous but inspiring boss.

> 'Come in Arthur and bring John with you. Lads I have an important project which I want done properly. That is why I have asked you and John Tiffney to do it. We're pushed for time but I know I can depend on you two. It will be rugged, it will be arduous, it'll be freezing but it will immortalise the pair of you. You know the rules. Always do a job in the certain knowledge that in one hundred years time those who look at your work will admire it.'

John Tiffney, my apprentice, glanced across at me. We both smiled.

> 'O.K. Harry,' I said, 'Time to reveal what fankle we are about to get our selves into?'

'Arthur, lad, you and Tiffney are my secret weapon. The top brass of the NCB all know of this job. It was they who dreamt it up. That is why I have chosen you pair- Little and Large- to do it.'

'Arthur, I think we should nip out the office and offer up three Hail Mary's before Harry divulges what he's up to.' sighed Tiffney.

Harry burst into a fit of the giggles. When he stopped he said:

'Lads, it's the coldest winter on record. We have snow up to the hedge tops, the wind chill for this month is the fiercest this century and all these stupid buggers at headquarters can think of is that it would be nice if they could be invited down to Monktonhall Colliery on Christmas Eve to officially switch on the Christmas lights. I know they're bonkers lads, but we'll play along with them.'

'But, Harry, where do you want us to put up these Christmas lights?' I asked.

Harry took off laughing again. When he got himself gathered he spluttered.

'On top of No 2 Tower! Yes, two hundred and twenty feet up in the pitch black! They want to be seen as participating in Harold Wilson's hi-tech revolution.' Harry raised his eyebrows in despair. 'It's a monument to their empty heads, idle hands and lazy arses.'

When the laughter eased young Tiffney yelled.

'Yes, yes. Harry!

Arthur, you and I could make a right go of this. Yes! Yes! I've just worked out that my granny will see it from her wee house in Mayfield three miles away. She'll know I did it and she'll write to all her friends in Australia to boast about me, her grandson, the illustrious John Tiffney. Harry, I'm up for it.'

'Arthur', Harry said 'You're just twenty three. You are twenty years younger than me. You can withstand the rigours of the weather. You and young Tiffney here could do this job on the end of your……screwdriver. What about it, will you do it? Oh, I must tell you that it can only be done each day between two in the afternoon and ten o'clock at night.'

'Harry, as the partridge said to the duck, if you're game then so am I. I'm beginning to see the comical side of all this. Let's welcome Christmas 1964 with a bang.'

We surveyed the flat roof of No 2 tower which straddled the pit shaft. We could anchor the lights to the three foot safety rail.

'Tiffney, I'm telling you, you had better dig out a pair of your dad's long–johns. That wind would cut you in half. Now, we've been up here ten minutes and I feel like the proverbial pawnbrokers sign.'

'Well, Arthur, I'm no as posh as that. I just feel my chuckies are clinking like pints in the pub. I can hear them play Amazing Grace.'

'No, John Tiffney, you are dreaming of a night playing with that amazing Grace Brownlee from the wages office!'

The Christmas lights came in four feet sections. We sussed that much of the preparatory work could be done in the warmth of the workshop. We made a fused distribution panel, shaped the mounting brackets, assembled and fitted a cable harness to each of the twenty-nine sub modules.

The Artic blast at the tower top awaited us. Harry dropped by so see how we were faring.

> 'Now, Tiffney lad, don't do to poor Arthur what I did to him yesterday.'

'You gave him a new roll of insulating tape for his birthday. Didn't you?' Tiffney quipped.

'No, it was much worse than that. It was just so innocently done.' said Harry.

'I sent him to shift the power supply on the top of No1 Tower for the contractors. He went up but had to wait till they finished at four o'clock and of course darkness was falling. They all came down the temporary lift and the last man locked it off without thinking of Arthur who was two hundred feet up on top of the tower with no way of getting down.'

Arthur finished the swap at half past six. His lamp was down to a glimmer. An icy gale was howling and there he was stuck up there for the night with no shelter and no food and no warmth.

Nobody could see him. No one could hear him and worst still I forgot he was even up there.

I rushed back to work and set off to get him. He had clambered down two hundred feet of scaffolding, carrying his tool bag, in the pitch dark. But it ran out twenty feet from the ground on his side of the tower. That is where I spotted him.

I shouted to him.

'Arthur, if you can get round to my side I'll get a ladder.'

'Thanks. Harry there's a ledge that I can jump on to. It'll get me round and down to the ground.'

'I got back with the ladder but he was just standing in the same place.'

'What's up Arthur?' I hollered.

'Harry, I've lost all my tools.'

'How did you manage that?'

'Harry, I threw my tool bag on to that ledge before I jumped onto it. My tools just disappeared three thousand feet down the pit shaft.'

'How?'

'Because that ledge was a shadow, Harry, that's how!'

With two days to go we humped all our gear and the modules to the roof top of Number 2 Tower. Wrapped in donkey jackets, scarves and balaclavas we battled against the searing icy wind. A labourer had organised a coal brazier on the floor below. We worked for five minutes then raced down to thaw out our finger tips, then rattled upstairs to work for another five minutes till we perished again.

On Christmas Eve, Simon Kidlaw, the chief regional electrical engineer, called down to the workshop floor:

> 'Now can I get you chaps a well earned drink for your Christmas?'

'No thanks, It's most kind of you' I said. 'Naw, Tiffney and I are off to midnight Mass now. We daren't go pissed.'

Harry who was standing in the shadows beckoned to me and Tiffney.

> 'You know' he whispered 'They think we've put up a temporary Christmas tree with fairy lights. They'll cut my head off when they see what you have done and what I've spent.'

John Gibson, the group electrical engineer was a decent bloke whom the tradesmen all liked, stepped forward towards us.

'I think we should ask these two brave chaps to do us the honour. Will you do it?'

'Tiffney and I think Harry should do it.' I chimed. Harry threw the switch.

Ants and angels were startled to suddenly see a large brilliant new light appear, as though suspended, in the dark starless sky. For miles, it beamed its presence to the world.

MONKTONHALL COLLIERY

Thus was the coming of the light, and Christmas, for John Tiffney's granny.

Part Three

My Dad was my hero. It was he who had taught me, as a schoolboy, the magic of planting early potatoes, furrowing up the drills then digging the first of them.

Ah, Mince and Epicure tatties in August followed the next evening with a poke of home made chips!

Celestial, nay, glorious, feasts for all of our large working class family and our neighbours too!

About that time Jocky Broon walked home from a flower show with a swathe of gladiolas across his arms and silver cups dangling from his fingers.

'Oh, God. 'I thought 'If only I could do that.'

I wanted too but I couldn't. I did not even know where to start. He must have mystical powers or be inveigled in some kind of secret society of champion growers. Why was everything that my dad and I grew just normal or small or pallid and Jocky's were always large, vibrant and colourful? Thirty five years later, by good fortune, I met Willie Tear the renowned Garvald gardener. It was he who unleashed a great torrent of gardening advice upon me. He taught me how to grow and to show. Through him I was introduced into the realms of horticultural societies and flower shows and those good, honest and comical folk who run them.

I also collided with a tiny number of exhibitors; There were those who strung two bunches of green grapes together, so cleverly, with green string; Those who entered apples that were known to grow only in South Africa; Those who displayed roses reared only in Nigeria; Those who used a distinctive name tab to identify their entry of chrysanths claiming it was to educate the public rather than tip off the judge; Those who showed Iceberg lettuces from Mrs Tesco's Shop; Those whose bakery produce had the baker's name embedded into its base; Those who entered a hand knitted jumper with the makers label intact; And all for the sake of a first prize of £1. And always the same few exhibitors! Not to forget the soul whom I saved from the lynch mob after he absconded with our society's funds!

The converse was true of show manager, Dougie Neill. He spotted an entry with five jam scones. The class called for only four. To avoid the judge disqualifying that lady, Dougie, an honest and thoughtful fellow simply scoffed the fifth!

After twenty-eight years in which we have sought to spread the interest in growing and showing it is time for me now to recognise the true worth of my competitors on the show bench. In these following stories I salute my fellow sons of the soil!

Jim Kirkness
Jacky Davidson and Jim Williams
Davy Grindlay and Sally Farmer
Scotland's finest growers, judges and exhibitors.

Phallic Symbolism

All my life I've been troubled with elderly aristocrats. They just cannot accept that there's so few folk left for them to control.

Dod Ferguson and I agreed, in 1984, to establish the Garvald Onion and Leek Society. Within a short period we had a membership of twenty-four. We formed a committee, created a constitution and listed a selection of novel classes and all with fair rewards. We aimed to develop the knowledge of horticulture within the membership, many of whom had neither grown vegetables nor competed before.

Our first show was held in the village hall and was heralded with much fanfare aided by local press photographs. Two weeks later, I was standing in Haddington watching the world go by when Lady Linplum struck! This country lady, with brown brogues, tweed skirt, green Pringle twin set, armless anorak and blue rinsed hair bore down upon me. Prodding my chest repeatedly, she screeched.

'I know about your kind, Mr Greenan. I know about you and your perverted friends, and don't you deny it!'

'Whoa! Whoa! I begged her to simply explain what she was raving on about.

'I saw you and your friends posing in The Courier photos, she thundered. You were all smiling and leering, like middle-aged creeps.'

'And' she went on. 'I know why you and your friends grow those mammoth onions. I know. It is plain vulgarity. And don't you dare tell me you are trying to improve horticulture.' She was by now florid and panting heavily.

'Tell me two things, my dear, how would you like if I prodded your chest and, please explain to me what is causing you such distress?'

'You damn well know why I'm upset and you know damn fine why you all grow those large onions.'

'No, I don't know why.'

'Oh yes. We all know about your kind.' She insisted.

'O.K. Enlighten me!'

She threw her forearms into the air with her hands cusped and gyrating at great speed she said.

'That is why. That is why. Phallic symbolism! Phallic symbolism!' she declared.

Astonished, I said 'Phallic what?'

'Phallic symbolism, you know full well what I mean. Mammary glands! Mammary glands! That's why you lecherous little gardeners grow them.'

'Lady Linplum, pray tell me this, what do people like you make of old Willie Tear who grows long carrots?'

Appalled, Lady Linplum stormed off!

Judge Laurie Tinderwood

As darkness fell I was having difficulty in the show tent telling my yellow chrysanthemums from the cream ones. Not only was the artificial light deceptive but I had also mislaid my spectacles. The Dalkeith Flower Show was being staged the next day in this large khaki marquee which was lit only by one sixty-watt bulb. Having placed all my entries on the show bench I still had three spare blooms left.

> 'Put them in they are good enough, they will bump up your points as well as adding to the competition.'

Someone shouted.

The class called for three incurved chrysanthemums of the same breed and colour, so in they went! When the show opened on Saturday afternoon I ran round to the chrysanthemum section. There, within this magnificent tiered array of prize-winning entries, was my vase with three blooms of World of Sport. And lo, there too was the First Prize ticket. Exhibiting against quality growers of chrysanthemums, I had won one First Prize. I was chuffed about it but not about my vase of yellow Primrose Cricket chrysanthemums. It had been disqualified!

Nevertheless, I stood soaking up the beauty of a rainbow of varieties, Kimberly Marie, Billy Bell, Eve Gray, Pearl Celebration, Rachael Knowles and Lorna Wood. It was then a small balding fellow, who was listing slightly to the port side, stumbled into me.

'Got anything in.' the man asked.

'I have indeed,' I said pointing proudly: 'See that cracking vase of World of Sport, well, those are mine.'

'And who are you?'

'Oh, I'm just a learner.' I replied.

'Oh, I'm Laurie Tinderwood. I'm the flower judge. I'm a bit tipsy now, I've had a long day but if I can give you any advice just ask.'

I opened my show programme and read the names of the officers. Laurie Tinderwood was Secretary, Treasurer, Show manager and Minutes secretary. Little wonder the man looked a bit ragged. What a game sort, I thought, as I turned to question him.

'Always glad to help a keen beginner,' said Laurie.

'What happened to this entry, why did you disqualify it Mr Tinderwood?' I asked

'Good chrysanths but the wrong bloody mix.' He said. 'He's got a good vase of blooms but has mixed in the Primrose Cricket variety with the Ginger Nut variety. They're close in colour, close in shape, close in size but they're just not the same chrysanths. The programme called for three identical chrysanthemums. They are not identical! That's why. Whose entry is it anyway?' Mr Tinderwood glowered, and shuffled unsteadily.

I lifted up the entry card and knowing that it was my own, turned it over and read out the competitor's name.

'It was put in by a chap called Arthur Greenan. That's the name on this class card.'

The judge muzzled up to me and whispered.

'Do you know this Greenan fellow?'

Yes, I know him very well. I've known him all my born days. I knew his mother, father, brothers and sisters too.'

Arthur Greenan with the variety, Billy Bell.

'Well, the next time you see the stupid bugger tell him he could do a lot better if he got himself a new pair of specs, was a bit more vigilant and less careless too. Will ye do that, son?'

'Yes, Mr Tinderwood, I'll tell him the next time I see him.'

As we shook hands and parted I smiled. I had heard the truth. Just as half-pissed judges tell it.

The Honorarium

Bob Johnston had spent the whole of his working life with East Lothian Water Board. In the beginning he dug holes. He then supervised others in the art of digging holes. In time Bob rose to become the clerk to various sub-committees yet he never lost touch with the workers from whence he came. Such was the esteem in which Bob was held that when he retired that the head of the Water Board and all their manual workers were invited to a social evening in his honour.

After a fair skelp of whisky and a sumptuous meal, Councillor Willie Waterson, Chairman of the Water Board, mounted the podium. He called to Bob to his side. He then recalled Bob's great skill, his leadership, his compassion and his legendary Christmas flings. It was then that he produced a brown envelope.

> 'Bob Johnston, I ask you on behalf of the people of East Lothian, the staff and the workers of East Lothian Water Board to accept this honorarium as a token of our great respect for you.'

Bob glanced at the envelope stuffed with pound notes and gasped.

'Bugger me' he declared, 'I always thought that an honorarium was a pot plant!'

A Rose by Any Other Name

*Greater love hath no man than trounce his neighbour
at their parish Flower Show*

I raced in to catch the last five minutes of the Flower Show held in the Esk Valley College at Dalkeith. The car park by was now empty. I strolled in solitude around the tables of the vegetable section viewing exhibits grown by Scotland's finest gardeners. The highlight at Dalkeith Show is the array quality roses entered. Such breathtaking produce, so brilliantly displayed, is really all that any gardener could aspire to.

As I turned into the floral hall the Dalkeith Horticultural Society committee had formed itself into two opposing tribes both of whom who were hurling abuse at each other across the table. Swearwords of the most expressive kind cracked the evening air. Witnessing this rammy from a slight distance, but unseen, I worked out that the conflict arose about the proper name of a blue rose.

In a flash two words inexplicably came to mind-

Vox Populi. Thirty years earlier I had purchased my first bicycle in Musselburgh and the transfer on the crossbar bore those two latin words; *Vox Populi*. As the barrage of insults escalated so too did the intensity of the anger in their voices. As I drew level to them there was a momentary hush. It was then I pointed to this perfectly formed blue rose and jubilantly declared.

'Ah, that's *Vox Populi!*'

The warriors were stunned into silence.
I moved on without a backward glance. As I disappeared among the tall gladioli and large chrysanthemums I was accosted by the show manager. He was small, rotund and balding with twenty-three badges on his blazer lapels and fourteen Biro pens in his top pocket.

'Hey, Jimmy. Hey, Jimmy. Come here. Come here.' He insisted

I recoiled at the thought of this little pugilist thinking that I was some kind of rose expert. He was amazed that I knew the name of the blue rose and begged me to write it down for him on the back of his fag packet which I did.

'What was its name again?' He demanded.

'Does it really matter?' I asked him.

'Of course it f*****g matters. This is serious, Son!' He rasped.

> 'Well, that blue beauty was *Vox Populi*, which means voice of the people' I replied.

As he left he walloped my back with a hearty slap.

> 'See you, Jimmy, you are a star. Thanks pal.
> Thanks a million. See that bloody woman up there, her that is doing all the yapping, she has shown that rose at this Show for twenty-eight years and never even knew its flaming name!'

So, should you ever set eyes on that beautiful blue rose please remember that its name was inspired, not by my 1956 Raleigh bike alone but by the fechting members of Dalkeith Flower Show Committee.

Bless them all!

The Canon and the Curate

A new curate arrived in the mining town of Tranent in 1960. Father Michael Cassidy, yet to hit thirty years of age had been sent to ease the parochial travails of old Canon Murphy and to build a new church as well.
Could it be done and could he do it?

It was bewildering to meet this priest who was young, welcoming and in tune with the lives of most souls in the town. With his engaging sense of humour the parishioners soon rallied to him. I spotted his car outside our house. The visit to my mother was threefold; He shared her love of poetry; enjoyed her home-baked scones; and was in need of his socks which she had just darned.

'Chum me down the road, Arthur?' He asked.

'I'll just get my coat.'

'I need your help old son.' He said ,as we strolled down Haddington Road.

'The parishioners are ashamed of the sight of their old wooden church. If I spruce up the garden until such times as we get a new church built it will be a great help. Will you help me?'

'Father, you decide what you think you need, tell me about it and I will tell you what is possible. It's a dreadful mess but let's go for it.'

The whole ambience of St Martin of Tours church when he had arrived was that of decay. The main street formed the southern boundary of a square. The original stone-built church had collapsed. It had lasted only ten years having been built on wobbly ground. When the plaster, defying the hand of God, hit the foreheads of the parishioners at prayer it was decided it must close.

The existing wooden church which was constructed of weather-boarding in the style of a Dutch hen-house was built in 1938. Sanctity and deep spirituality were wrought from the parishioners through penance. It was mental and physical torture to attend Mass in that wooden church. The Canon conducted his whole litany at breakneck speed in Latin, all of which shot over the heads of his working class parishioners. They responded to prayers which they simply did not understand. It was loyalty engrained by fear and prayers recited by rote. In winter draughts seeped through the slits in the floor and straight up your trouser leg. The heating system was never proven to work. Canon Murphy was never found guilty of buying coal. But the sword of Damocles - mortal sin - ensured our weekly attendance as passive recipients of a dogma which, to most of us, was quite incomprehensible.

The overgrown church garden looked like a haunted house. The straggly privet hedge hid the church house from public view. The rose bushes had returned to briar and the lawn to hay. This suited the reclusive Canon but not the gregarious Cassidy. Father Michael gutted what he could of the garden without triggering the full ire of his boss. In a few months he and I had created a delightful lawn bordered with the white, blue and lemon of alyssum, lobelia and tagetes. But still that forbidding hedge remained. He dithered as to how he should effect a reduction in height and what the likely reaction of the old battleaxe Murphy would be.

One Friday morning as Canon Murphy shuffled down to the fish shop, I nipped in and sawed out a three foot gap, bang in the middle of the hedge, then fled for home.

'Hell hath no fury like the Canon Murphy's and scorn.' But he conceded and the rest of the hedge was lowered. Archbishop Gordon Gray aggravated the Canon too by insisting on being photographed with newly-weds in the middle of Father Cassidy's new lawn.

A few days after I had ambushed that hedge, I caught up with Father Cassidy who was on his way to collect the unemployment benefit for a seriously ill parishioner. As we parted I met a neighbour who was standing opposite the dole office waiting his on friends coming out to repay him the tick they were due him for their drink.

'Arthur, who's that?' he asked as the curate disappeared into the dole office.

'That's the new priest, Father Cassidy.' I said.

My friend, who seriously believed that the young priest was about to collect his own dole money, shook his head in utter despair.

'God, things are bad, eh? Look at that, even the Pope's paying them off!'

On the evening of Thursday, 11th November 1999, I had gone to Tranent to attend a meeting, not connected with the church, but normally held in their hall. The meeting was cancelled. The hall was laid out for a buffet. The church lights were on. Having driven twelve miles I thought, rather than waste the evening, I would just catch the remainder of the Mass. I slipped in quietly and found a seat at the back. Who was conducting a concelebrated Mass with clergymen from all other denominations but Michael, now Canon, Cassidy. They were marking thirty years of ownership of the new St Martin of Tours church by the parishioners.

I looked around and saw a few people with whom I had started at infant school with fifty years earlier. Then I thought of those gardening episodes with Cassidy thirty-five years ago, and smiled. I reflected too on our campaign in 1970 against the brutality unleashed upon the Irish potato-pickers by their own bosses. All these events tiptoed across my mind.

At the end of the Mass these multi-denominational clergymen walked in procession around the perimeter aisle.

I shook hands in silence with Michael Cassidy as he passed. I then remembered how, many years ago, I had lain retching at the gates of Hell, how Father Cassidy had picked me up and shunted me back between the tracks and how, by the grace of God, I had managed to stay there.

Some pal!
Some day!
Some pair!

The Roses of Haddington

I've often wondered if the end ever justifies the means and if dishonesty belongs only in a large city and not in a rural market town like Haddington. Not so it seems.

It floored Jim McGregor, the mechanic, to discover that a country engineer like him, whose livelihood relied on his technical competence and fair play, could be screwed too by his local customers.

He had started out on his own as an agricultural engineer in the early fifties. Farmers with clapped out tractors relied upon the skills of forty-year old Jim. A brigade of brickies, plumbers and joiners begged Jim to breathe life back into their knackered vans so that they may last for just one more year. So too did the market gardener, Bill Gourlay.

> 'So Jim, did Mr Gourlay ever pay you for sorting his truck?'
>
> 'Never did Bob. And he's the fellow that told everybody how pleased he was with my work. He said that I had it pulling like a shunting engine. He's a two-faced

robbing swine. That was two years ago, but how do you get your money back from scallywags like that?'

'How much is he still due ye Jim?'

'Twenty-five quid Bob, without the interest added.'

'Heavens, Jim, that's three weeks wages for a man!'

'Ah know Bob, I don't suppose I'll ever see a brass farthing o' it now. You see, Gourlay knows fine that for me to take him to the court would cost me more in legal fees than that twenty-five quid he is due me.'

'Jim is there not another way to skin a cat?' said Bob.

'But how, Bob? That is the question.'

'Well, it's a long shot but it's the kind of ruse that I would try without any compunction. So if you want to have a go Jim, I'll help you.'

'Bob if you've got the guts to help I'll find the courage too. So, where now?'

'Jim, in Haddingtonshire Courier this week Mr Gourlay is advertising a big rose sale in his yard tomorrow.'

'How much are they apiece Bob?'

'Two shillings and sixpence a bush, or twelve and a half pence or eight rose bushes to the pound. That's not bad for a Blue Moon or a Fragrant Cloud or a decent Harry Wheatcroft rose now is it Jim?'

'And they're all hybrid teas, Bob?'

'They are that, Jim. Why not get your wife a couple to replace those two that got frosted?'

'I wouldn't buy a second hand bike from that man never mind roses. No, I better not. She'd just faint! Jane is a hard working woman Bob; I feel that he has stolen from her as well as me. It was her money that helped me get started in business.'

'Jim, come on now. The age of chivalry is not yet dead. And neither are you.'

'I wished that Gourlay knew about chivalry! Bob. He has just no conscience at all.'

'Jim, forget about Gourlay just now. We'll sort him! Get Jane a couple of rose bushes for the front gate. Ye might even get a wee peck for your trouble.'

'Now, that could be rare, Bob.

The two friends then seriously set about devising a plan to retrieve the twenty five pounds which Gourlay had stolen from him Jim. Theft by keeping was their judgement. But how could they trump Gourlay's card without arousing his suspicion. Bob suggested that Jim recruit his wife Jane. Jane thanked Jim warmly for the surprise of a lovely bouquet of red and white picotee carnations.

'Jane, come here sweetheart I've got a wee job for you.

Now just concentrate. This is our plan.'

Jane didn't flinch. She had the character and the will to carry off his daring little deed. She took in a deep breadth as she entered the market garden yard the next morning.

'Hello Mr Gourlay, you're having a rose sale I see?'

Oh, it's you Mrs McGregor. Yes, I've got some good rose bushes for sale. How many do ye fancy?'

'I hope you don't think I'm daft Mr Gourlay but I'm not too sure, it could be two or it could be two hundred. We could actually get five-hundred into our garden if we lifted the lawn and sacrificed the vegetable garden. I can just see a blaze of colour covering our south facing slope.'

'Quick. Come round to the back shed. I've some real toppers stacked here, good quality too!'

'Mr Gourlay, how much are they apiece?' Jane asked.

'Half a crown or twelve and a half pence if you are on decimal '

'But, if I bought fifty?'

'Two bob.'

And, if I bought two-hundred?'

'One shilling and sixpence apiece, how's that for a bargain?'

'I'll tell ye what, if you'll settle for a shilling apiece I'll buy five hundred.'

'Why not! On ye go then missus.'

'I could give you a cheque for £25 right now for the lot.'

'Thank you Mrs McGregor and thanks for the prompt payment. It's been grand doing business with you.'

Jane took two hundred rose bushes to her work at the Roodlands Hospital. Jim set up a table in the bus park at East Fortune Sanatorium. By Saturday evening they had, between them, sold three hundred bushes to visitors and staff. On Sunday, Jane pitched her table at Herdmanflat Hospital and Jim set out his roses at the Vert Hospital. By sunset they had, sold all of the five-hundred, one-shilling rose bushes for two shillings and sixpence each.

Jim arrived to find the back door open:

'Jane, darling, are you in?'

'Yes sweetheart!'

'Come out here you devastatingly clever and beautiful wee woman I've got something special for you.'

He removed the latch of the garden shed door, led her inside.

Later over a celebratory glass of wine in the kitchen Jim said:

'Well done, Jane. You're a wizard. That gives us a clear profit of £37 and 10/-. But, there is more, much more, my little rose.'

'Aw. No, Jim. Not another five hundred rose bushes.'

'No. No, darling, much less demanding and then a candlelit dinner will be yours, my beautiful little wife.'

At 10 o'clock sharp on Monday morning Jane McGregor slipped into the Clydesdale bank in Court Street.

'Could you kindly tell me if you have you received the cheque that I made out in favour of Mr Gourlay yet?'

'Indeed we have.'

'Just cancel it, please.'

The Cardinal's Cucumber

Did Cardinal Gordon Gray commit a venial sin or did he not? That is the question!

The village of Garvald lies by the Papana Water, hidden in a sheugh at the foot of the Lammermuir Hills in the heart of East Lothian. It is the home of the Cistercian Monks at Sancta Maria Abbey. The abbey sod was cut in 1952 and over the next seventeen years the new monastery was built with Rattlebag whinstone laid by the hand of the master stonemason, former prisoner of war and raconteur William Tear.

Among the many hundreds from secular, religious and academic worlds who flocked to build Sancta Maria there was none to whom Willie deferred. Not even the Archbishop of St Andrew's and Edinburgh, Cardinal Gordon Joseph Gray. From their very first meeting it was the cut and thrust of a good argument which always ended by one trying to the trump the other's card.

Willie liked the Cardinal. He admired his implacable humanitarianism but despaired at his political conservatism. Cardinal Gray trusted Willie's instincts though he was quite mystified to find that a manual worker could be so well read. Thus the die for many a serious joust between them was cast. Visits to Willie and Elizabeth's home were the Cardinal's antidote to his role as an international statesman and shepherd of his national flock. It was his hiding place. A good log fire, the carpet slippers on, a nip of whisky in hand and a good crack with Willie, was as close to Heaven as the Cardinal could find on this turbulent earth.

Their relationship blossomed when they discovered a love of propagating flowers and vegetables from seed. The Archbishop and the artisan sought to out-fox each other in horticultural knowledge too.

When I first met Willie in the early summer of 1980 he was disbudding his show chrysanthemums. Without raising his head, Willie pounced.

'You won't be a socialist. Will you?'

I rocked back on my heels, took a deep breath then counterattacked.

'I certainly am if you really must know I'm a bloody pape too!'

Willie smiled and stretched out his hand.

'There's absolutely nothing wrong with that. I am so pleased to meet a kindred spirit. You know, there is not many of my kind up here. Most of them strive to get close to God, but me, I'd rather see folk from a' these different countries join Jock Tamson's family. There wouldn't be any more wars after that son. Anyway, I had better give you some plants to get you started.'

'Willie, I've never grown a chrysanthemum in my life, never mind show them.'

'Well you have now - son. And don't worry, I'll keep you right.'

Two years later we formed The Garvald Onion and Leek Society, enrolling twenty-three members.

'It's twenty-four now,' Willie informed the meeting.

'Been canvassing again Willie?' asked the president.

'No, new recruits flock to my door. If you really must know, our newest member is His Eminence Cardinal Gray. Just give me a membership card and you can have his fiver. You see, ye didn't know I had influential friends in high places. Now, did ye Dod? My friends are even close to God which is more than you bloody reprobates can claim!'

'Mr Tear, I did not know that now.' Replied Dod Ferguson, the president.

Whilst still fully ambulant, that the Cardinal exhibited at Garvald Flower Show of which Willie was the show manager. On the Saturday morning of the show I had shuttled the last of Willie's fifty two entries down to the village hall. At ten o'clock the hall was cleared of exhibitors just before the judges arrived.

Willie, lifting his bonnet said:

'Well, Arthur, there's nothing we can do now but let's give them all the entries one last quick check just in case.'

We relocated three entries to their proper place. Having sorted the floral sections, we turned into the vegetable sections. Therein lay a beautiful silver salver with picket fence edging holding two matching cucumbers. Well, one was of normal size, the other the size of a wee crinkly Walls sausage!

'Christ Almighty!' blurted Willie. 'Who would enter a thing like that?'

'We'll soon find out Willie.'

Turning the entry card over I said. 'It's your old pal, Willie.'

It's who?'

'Willie, it's your famous old pal.'

'Oh. No, oh No. Not the Cardinal.'

'Yes, Willie, you're dead right!'

'Quick. Quick before the judges come. Quick now!'

I sped up the hill, raced into his glasshouse and rocketed back down whizzing past the judges. I rattled into the hall and pocketed the wizened morsel. I then placed the new cucumber beside the Cardinal's good one.

It was a matter of great pride that day for Willie to be asked to chum the Cardinal around the Show. It was, for Gordon Joseph, pleasurable too to meet the people he truly liked amongst the flowers he truly loved. Conscious of their slow pace, I suggested that we all meet up later in the tea tent. Their propensity to discuss every exhibit, in detail with everyone, left little time for the cup of tea. The Cardinal was now late for prayers and had left for the monastery.

Legless, Willie had been ambushed by the giggles. He rolled into the tea tent and clung to the centre pole, still giggling.

'You'll never guess what happened? Arthur.

> We got to his salver and he asked me what the cup was for and why he had won it. So I told him that it was for his cucumbers which were the best two cucumbers in the Show. I also told him that he had a first–prize ticket

to go with the cup as well. The old boy then turned to me.'

'Are you sure about this Willie?'

'Of course I'm sure about the result but if you're not happy see the judges. Your Eminence this has bugger-all to do with me! Well, Cardinal Gray put then his arm around my shoulder and whispered.

'You know, Willie, The Lord does work in mysterious ways!'

Gordon Joseph Gray, Cardinal, was born on 10th August in Leith, 1910. He died in Edinburgh on 19th July, 1993, aged 82 yrs and is buried in St Mary's Cathedral, Edinburgh..

Willie Tear, stonemason, was born on 6th May in Dunbar, 1915. He died at Nunraw, November, 15th, 1998, aged 83 yrs and is buried beside Elizabeth Violet Tear at Sancta Maria Abbey, Garvald, East Lothian

Ladybird

The picturesque village of Gifford is the place at which the crème de la crème of gardeners display their produce. I was urged one year, to exhibit my sweet peas at the annual flower show on the village green. The show opened at two o'clock and I raced in with great expectations.

There were eight vases of sweet peas on the show bench. In two of the vases the flowers, which were royal blue with a white picotee fringe, were stunningly beautiful and deserved first prize. Their presentation was sheer elegance, as were the other four vases. The two the remaining vases, without a prize ticket, were mine.

'Hello lad.' He spoke down to me from a great height.

'Got anything in the show?'

I didn't know that this elderly giant of a man was the legendary grower, George Scott from Oxton village in Berwickshire.

'Yes I have. Those are my two vases of sweet peas.'

'And did you win anything, Son?'

'I've got a fourth prize out of four, that's all. And little wonder looking at the quality of those two other vases. They make my sweet peas look drunk.' I replied.

'Have you got anything in the show?' I asked him.

'Aye, sweet peas, them's mine there with the first prize ticket and the cup. Are you interested in showing sweet peas?' Mr Scott asked.

'I certainly am!'

'Well, can I say this to you son, and I don't mean any offence to you in any way but you will never ever beat me showing rubbish like that!'

With that he held out his hand, shook mine and laughed.

'Now, I'm George Scott, I live in the village of Oxton.

We need younger folk like you to keep this tradition alive. You come up and see the wife and I and I'll teach you every thing you ever needed to know about sweet peas. I'll show you what seeds to plant and when. What feeding to give them and when to do it. I show you too how to train and trim them and above all how to prepare them for the show bench. Then we can have a right contest just between you and me!'

The next summer I was ready for George. I had followed his propagation procedures to the letter.

'Let battle commence.' I thought as I sprinted into the show marquee.

Four vases of sweet peas; his two and my two looked quite stunning. Placed at George's entry was the cup. Despondently I held out my hand to congratulate my mentor and worthy victor.

'Well George I tried every trick in the book and still you beat me!'

'No. No son, I haven't beaten you today. No, your flowers are as good as mine. You have done well today lad.'

'Just a pity Arthur Greenan cannot count.'

Chimed, the familiar voice of Alec Birse, the Flower Section judge.

'The rules, you daft sod, call for twelve flower stems in each vase. You, laddie can only count up to eleven. So there!' It was a great pity too because you had big George up against it on quality.'

Alec Birse, flower show judge

Alec Birse had the memory of an elephant. He turned to George Scott and I.

'Do you know what Greenan did twenty years ago at East Linton Flower Show, George? He entered a plate of shallots which were excellent. They were the Hative De Niort variety and were, supposedly, a perfectly matched dozen. Not his. He had only placed eleven on his plate and instead of winning a cup I had to disqualify his entry. Silly bugger!'

At the end of the showing season George and Mrs Scott set of on their annual holiday- a bus trip round the highlands and islands of Scotland. Whilst on tour they were approached by a middle-aged American and fellow traveller, Walter Huntly.

'Would you good folks mind if I sat with you.' Walter asked.

'Please do, son. Are you on your own.' asked George.

'Yes I am. My dear wife, Aimee, passed away suddenly six months ago.'

'Yes, I can understand how you are feeling. Aye, a boat without a rudder, I know how you feel. Please feel free to join us for dinner tonight as well. There is no need for you to be on your own, at least for the rest of this week.' added George.

Both men enjoyed a dram of whisky each night and a good crack about the history and the making of their respective countries. As the two men, George, a one time the ploughman and council roadman and Walter, the American consul, parted at the end of the trip they resolved to keep in touch.

A few weeks later the phone rang in Oxton village.

'Hello, may I speak with Mr George Scott the sweet pea man from bonnie Scotland.'

'Yes, George speaking.'

'George this is Lyndon. I'm a friend of Walter's. I grow sweet peas as well. Walter asked me to call you to ask if I could send you a new seed called Ladybird.' It's named after my wife. She likes it. It is a blue picotee.'

'Of course you can Lyndon. Please do. I'll be pleased to try it out. Tell me how is Walter?'

'George, Walter is sitting right here and he asked me to thank you and Mrs Scott for looking after him.'

'Oh, that is kind of him. He's a fine fellow, Lyndon. Do the pair of you work together then?'

'We used to George, but we're both retired now.'

'My, and what did you do for a living, Lyndon.'

'George, I used to be the President of the United States.'

Part Four

The inclusion of the stories of James Cameron and John P. Mackintosh may seem out of kilter with the content of the first three parts. Not so!

It was drummed into my four sisters, three brothers and I that all men and women were born equal in the eyes of God. And, according to our Dad, if that was good enough for God then it was good enough for any man no matter his station in this life.

Thus it became incomprehensible to us Scots that other human beings should be brutalised because of the colour of their skin as in Mr Cameron's story, or because of their timidity in the face of brutality as in the case of the Irish potato pickers or indeed the British miners who were who were crushed underfoot because of their political stance.
All it takes for thugs to succeed on this earth is for good men to do nothing. James Cameron didn't, he stood against the tide as indeed did John P. Mackintosh.

The Black Holocaust

James Cameron

Lynching survivor and founder of the Black Holocaust Museum

Born, 25th February, 1914, La Crosse, Wisconsin.
Died, 11th June, 2006, in Milwaukee, aged 92.

Obituary

As it appeared on 16th, June, 2006, in The Scotsman newspaper

The bruised and battered bodies of two young men hung from the limb of a maple tree. Between the corpses there was a space: wide enough for a black boy to be lynched, room enough for more death.

The space was intended for James Cameron.

That summer's night in 1930, the same mob that lynched his two friends came for Cameron. A noose was forced around the boy's neck. Voices called for his death.

Yet Cameron lived to tell the tale of that night in Marion, Indiana-and the story of the lynching in the United States well into the 21st century.

'They had a rope around my neck and they were going to rope me up between my two buddies. And I prayed to God.' Cameron said in an interview last year. *'I was saved by a miracle.'*

Cameron was known to be the nation's last known survivor of a lynching and whose brush with death fostered a lifelong commitment to civil rights that included the creation of America's Black Holocaust Museum.
Speaking with the unrivalled authority of a survivor, Cameron gave voice to history's untold number of lynching victim's, reminding the nation of this disgraceful page from its past was written not so long ago.

Before that night in 1930 Cameron was a shoeshine boy with no criminal record. He was in a car with two older friends - Thomas Shipp, 18, and Abe Smith, 19 - when they began to plan a robbery *'and like an idiot, I followed them,'* he said.

Shipp and Smith gave Cameron a gun and told him to rob a couple parked at Lovers Lane. Cameron tried but realised the man in the car was one of his shoeshine customers, Claude Deeter. Cameron gave the gun back and ran home, not stopping or turning back even after he heard gunshots.

Cameron and the two others were arrested a short time later.

The next day, Deeter died of wounds he suffered that night. Word of his death and the claim that his girlfriend had been raped spread and soon a huge mob formed. The enraged crowd broke into jail and dragged the boys out. From the window of his cell, Cameron watched the barbaric spectacle of his friends being beaten and lynched.

'They got Tommy, and they dragged him through the street like a dead horse,' he said.

Then they came back for Cameron. The mob beat the boy, spat on him. Kicked him and chanted for his death. Cameron looked into the faces of neighbours, people whose shoes he'd shined, *'and with whom I would pass the cordialities of the day.'* With the noose around his neck he prepared to die. Cameron described what happened next as divine intervention:

'And then a voice came down from heaven and said "Take this boy back. He had nothing to do with the killing or raping.'
Someone removed the noose, and the mob allowed him to stumble back to jail.

Eventually Deeter's girlfriend admitted that she had not been raped. After a year in jail, Cameron was convicted of being an accessory before the crime and served four years of a two-to-21 year sentence. No-one was convicted for the lynchings.

After his release at the age of 21, Cameron moved to Detroit, where he found work driving a truck for a laundry. On his route he met Virginia Hamilton, and the two married in 1938. The couple had five children. The family eventually moved back to Indiana where Cameron founded three chapters of the National Association for the advancement of coloured People and became president of the Madison County Branch in Anderson. For eight years, beginning in 1942, he served as the state's director of civil liberties, a position whose duties included reporting to the governor on violations of the 'equal accommodations' laws

When such work brought threats against his family, Cameron packed up his wife and children and set out for Canada, determined to leave America's racism behind. On the way he stopped in Milwaukee, liked the city and decided to make it the family's new home. The move marked a coming home for Cameron, who was born in La Crosse, Wisconsin, in 1914. In 1952, when he returned, racial injustice was still a fact of life in the state. He worked at a brewery in Milwaukee, and among other jobs, and became involved in protests to end housing segregation.

Growing up, the Cameron children knew little about their father's experience with lynching. When they were old enough he allowed them to read a manuscript about his life.

After an emotional 1979 visit to Yad Vashem, the museum in Israel that honours the millions killed in the

Holocaust, James Cameron decided to create a memorial to African Americans whose lives were lost to lynching, slavery and other injustices.

In 1988 on June 19-also known as the Juneteenth, the holiday commemorating the end of slavery in the US- the doors of America's Black Holocaust Museum opened.

The museum is housed in a 12000 square-foot building purchased from the city of Milwaukee for $1 and has operated on grants and donations. It houses a permanent exhibit on slavery, including a 15-foot reproduction of the cargo hold of a slave ship and a 45-foot enclosed mural depicting the journey from Africa across the Atlantic.

There is a series of photographs of lynchings and an exhibition on the Marion lynching, which included a piece of rope used in the killings and a now-infamous photo taken that night of Shipp and Smith hanging from a tree while a gleeful crowd mills about below. By the 1990s, Cameron's story had reached a wide audience through newspaper articles and television talk shows, including Larry King Live and Oprah. There was a documentary about the incident and plans for a movie about his life.

In June 2005, Cameron was present when the US Senate issued an apology for its failure to outlaw lynching. While some criticized the apology, Cameron was more circumspect: Yes, it was 100 years too late, he said, but he was glad to have it.

'I can forgive.' He often said, *'but I can never forget. That's why I started this museum.'*

James Cameron is survived by his wife, two sons, a daughter, five grand-children, six great-grandchildren and two great-great- grandchildren. Two of his sons predeceased him.

The Black Holocaust, an epilogue.

This letter was inspired by the obituary of Mr James Cameron and sent to the Curator of the Black Holocaust Museum, 2233, North Fourth Street, Milwaukee, Wisconsin, USA 53212

Dear Sir,
 James Cameron

Father, forgive them for they know not what they do!

Having read the obituary of your founder, Mr James Cameron, I felt impelled to send to you the copy which appeared in the *Scotsman* newspaper on Friday 10th June 2006.

I was deeply moved by this man's dedication to improving the lot of his fellow black citizen and also his exposure of man's inhumanity to man which, for decades, had made countless thousands mourn.

We Scots inadvertently laid the foundation of Mr Cameron's grief. We have given to the world some of its finest inventors, thinkers and philosophers.

We gave to America, James Wotherspoon, who formulated and signed the Declaration of Independence. He was born in the village of Gifford, East Lothian, Scotland.

We gave to America its most determined conservationist, John Muir, who created the Yellowstone and Yosemite parks. He was born in the small fishing town of Dunbar, East Lothian, Scotland.

We gave to the Confederate Army the sons of our finest Clydesdale horse–breakers. Driven from the farmland by mechanization their fathers faced city squalor or a new life in your country. They brought their skills of horse-whispering, learned in the secretive Society of Scottish Horsemen, to your land.

After the end of the American Civil War six young Confederate cavalry officers, of Scottish descent, decided, between Christmas 1865 and June 1866, to create a hellraising society to relieve their boredom. They were: James Crowe, Calvin Jones, John Kennedy, John Lester, Frank McCord and

Richard Reed. It was they who gave birth to the Ku Klux Klan. Tragically that organisation was hijacked by white supremacists who poured their illogical mental and physical putrefaction upon a people whose only sin was that they could be seen.

In Scotland today, and since the start of World War II when I was born, our children are taught to be bigoted against bigotry, to hate hatred and to be prejudiced against prejudice.

Scotland's national bard, Robbie Burns, inspires us too with this eternal hope:

> *Then let us pray, that come it may*
> *As come it will, for a' that*
> *That Man to Man, the world o'er*
> *Shall brithers be, for a' that*

I am pleased to have learned of Mr Cameron, a man whose political morality and instincts I readily support.

In America he had courage.

In England he had guts.

In Scotland he had smeddum!

Please kindly convey my most profound admiration of Mr Cameron and my most sincere condolences too for his loss to Mrs Cameron and their family.

Arthur Greenan   Sunday, 18th June 2007.

Prof. John P. Mackintosh MP

Ladies and gentlemen,

In paying tribute to the memory of John P. Mackintosh on this the 21st anniversary of his passing I have three abiding memories of John as, indeed, may all of you.

The first time I set eyes on John was when he and Councillor Andrew Purves were standing on the top step of Gifford village hall. Together they begged the passers-by to come into his first public meeting of the 1964 General Election campaign. That night he asked me to help him.

The second was of John striding fearlessly to the rostrum in Westminster Central Hall in 1971 then trying to persuade 5000 antagonistic people to embrace the principle of the Common Market when precious few of those present did, was memorable too. Despite the hollering and heckling, the barracking and the booing, he won their attention and then their admiration. Barbara Castle and Tony Benn were both moved by the emotional power of his argument, the brilliance of his oratory and his political honesty at a time when Labour shadow ministers were hiding in country mansion houses supping wine with Conservative ladies.

But, I ask myself, from whence doth inspiring men like Mackintosh come?

John Mackintosh resolutely believed, as did Robert Burns, that:

Man's inhumanity to man makes countless thousands mourn.

It was Robert Burns who inspired Scotland's finest philosopher, Thomas Carlyle from Ecclefechan. It was Carlyle, the Chartist, supported by his wife Jane Welsh from Haddington, who first embarrassed the middle class, then the upper class, then the aristocracy and then the monarchy of the day by exposing to them the dehumanising conditions that beset thousands of starving unemployed peasants in the countryside and millions more who dwelt in city squalor.

But, alas, nothing much happened for 50 years.

It was John Ruskin, inspired by Carlyle, who pressed those in government to put the competent artisan to work for the benefit of the country, and of their families. That was Social Democracy in its beginning. But, alas, little happened for another 50 years.

Until, one day in 1945, a man deeply influenced by Carlyle and Ruskin unexpectedly became Prime Minister. His name was Clement Atlee. At a stroke he created the welfare state. It was the most profound act of humanity by any government before or since.

It was in the wake of these revolutionary events that Scotland gave forth its finest ever clutch of inspired, young, political hopefuls. All were in the stamp of Ruskin and Carlyle; Tam Dalyell, Dickson Mabon, John Smith, Donald Dewar and the brightest of them all, John Pitcairn Mackintosh.

They were young men of personal courage and political conviction. They knew the high standards expected of them.

They understood the anguish of having political principles and of sticking to them. To a man, each had a burning desire to improve the lot of society to the harm and exclusion of none. Their every act was tinged with a touch of simple Christianity. They were all honest social democrats. Some quintet and all made in Scotland!

But how did John land on our doorstep? I'll give you just one example. As a young man he once launched a searing attack on the hydrogen bomb at the Scottish Labour Party conference only to be interrupted by the venerated chairman, Will Marshall:

'Son, we are hear to discuss Scottish affairs. Not hydrogen bombs. So, no more of that nonsense. None of that my lad!'

'But, isn't survival a Scottish affair?' Mackintosh pleaded.

Thus, John Mackintosh was forever marked down by the elderly Labour die-hards as a troublesome radical. Even the secret police in South Africa, who tailed him throughout his visit to their country in 1977, thought him to be a dangerous democrat too!

So, the Scottish Labour Party in despair, sent him to us—the hicks on the sticks—the simple minded country laddies of politics—and to contest the best run, most natural Conservative seat in the country. They assumed that he and his little helpers were bound to fail.

Dear God. If only they had known the inspiration of Mackintosh upon that little band.

Mackintosh was the original thinker, the enthusiastic educator, the incisive debater, the spellbinding orator, the acclaimed writer, the international parochialist, the amusing parliamentary mimic, but also the good and generous friend who inspired us to work for him.

A profound humanitarian, he was at his most lethal when defending those who always found themselves at the wrong end of every social stick.

Whatever you do to the least of my brethren you do unto me.

That was his simple philosophy. That was why we stuck with him.

And like Donald Dewar too he was a constitutional visionary whose electoral strength was anchored by the affection of his constituents. Without these two dogged and conscientious men, firstly Mackintosh, who campaigned relentlessly, followed later by Dewar, a Scottish Parliament would not have come to pass.

We remember too, the Trotskyites who passed this way. The destruction of John Mackintosh was their true intent. They had destroyed the political life of Dick Taverne M.P. in Lincoln and similarly, sought the demise of Berwick and East Lothian's M.P. They despised the Labour Party and found progressive social democrats like Taverne and Mackintosh anathema. They created mayhem within the constituency party. Some were councillors in East Lothian and Edinburgh others were minor academics. Some tried to use Mackintosh's pro-European stance to unseat him, others tried the Labour Party's constitution to lever him out. Neither group succeeded. It was John Mackintosh's band of littler helpers, of which I was but one, who saw to that and who put these nepotistic wreckers to flight.

John Mackintosh's productive intellect and boundless spirit confused Prime Ministers Harold Wilson and Jim Callaghan and Secretary of State for Scotland, Willie Ross. By their exclusion of Mackintosh, a man of unmistakable talent, we all know today how badly their governments, and this country, lost out. Even the noble lords, Jenkins, Owen and Rodgers ducked out of commending John for ministerial office albeit these same people knowingly picked his brains to their own advantage. Yet, in time, Harold Wilson wrote to me and Willie Ross told me, that in retrospect, to exclude John Mackintosh from ministerial office was wrong.

My third and most poignant memory of John was in July 1978. I had gone to cut his grass. John, who never spoke of the true extent of his condition, was by this time desperately ill. From that night when we had first met in Gifford all those years ago we had always parted with great bonhomie and a warm handshake.

He was sitting in his garden, with a straw hat, in the setting sun. That evening we shook hands, smiled and parted. Not a word was said. A few days later in the Western General hospital his jacket slipped silently from its shooglie nail.

His mighty heart was still.

Introductory address given by Arthur Greenan, founder at the annual John P. Mackintosh Memorial Lecture, Haddington, 1999, in the presence of Donald Dewar, the first ever First Minister of Scotland.

The End